NEVER BREAK THE CHAIN

FLEETWOOD MAC
and the making of RUMOURS

Also available in this series:

NEVER BREAK THE CHAIN
FLEETWOOD MAC
and the making of RUMOURS

CATH CARROLL

CHICAGO
REVIEW
PRESS

An A Cappella Book

Published by A Cappella Books
an imprint of Chicago Review Press, Incorporated
814 North Franklin Street
Chicago, Illinois 60610

Published by arrangement with Unanimous Ltd
12 The Ivories, 6–8 Northampton Street, London N1 2HY

ISBN: 1-55652-545-1

Printed in China

1 2 3 4 5 6 7 8 9

Picture credits

Cover, picture section page 1, 4 bottom, and 7 top left: © Fin Costello/Redferns. 2 top: © Araldo di Crollalanza/Rex Features; bottom: © Ivan Keeman/Redferns. 3 top: © Harry Goodwin/Rex Features; bottom, 4 top, and 5 bottom: © Neal Preston/Corbis. 5 top: © Deborah Feingold/Getty Images. 6: © Roger Ressmeyer/Corbis. 7 top right: © Barry Schultz/Camera Press; bottom: © Michael Ochs Archives/Redferns. 8 © Bettmann/Corbis.

Note: Every effort has been made to contact copyright holders; the editor would be pleased to hear from any copyright holders not acknowledged above.

contents

Dedication

For KK and Tabs.

introduction

The blues-rock band known to the world as Fleetwood Mac woke up one morning in February 1974 to the news that it was touring the United States again. A well-informed rock fan would find nothing unusual about that; the band's members had already established themselves as devoted road hounds. They performed live at every opportunity, often just for the fun of it. Live shows, which have often been seen by record companies as a waste of time unless they promote something, were this band's raison d'être. The members of Fleetwood Mac lived to make music, connect with the audience, and, with luck, make a little cash along the way.

The trouble was, Mick Fleetwood, John McVie, Christine McVie, and Bob Welch were anywhere but on tour. They were variously in Hawaii, Los Angeles, England, and Africa. Mick Fleetwood, after seven years of virtually nonstop touring and recording with the band, had been temporarily felled by a personal crisis involving his wife and a recently expelled member of the band. As a result, he and the other members of the band had told their longtime manager, Clifford Davis, that they would be taking a break. For the first time in their history, confirmed tour dates would have to be rescheduled. Davis, however, was determined to meet what he saw as his obligation to put a band called Fleetwood Mac on the road. And he did just that. Since the originals were not available, he put a group of under-rehearsed unknowns on tour. Obviously, Davis's concept of the band's essential identity differed from that of the real Fleetwood Mac and their audience. The "new" Fleetwood Mac tour proved to be a bad move for all concerned, including its unfortunate members, who were under the impression that at least one genuine Mac member would join them. They were not prepared for the hostility that greeted them on that short-lived, disastrous tour.

There was worse to come. The real Fleetwood Mac's subsequent dispute with Davis resulted in its suspension from playing and recording in the United Kingdom. The band's income stream dwindled, and things at the band's communal residence, Benifold, were grim indeed. Davis told them he owned Fleetwood Mac. The band would have to go to court to get their band name—and their lives—back. For Fleetwood Mac was more than just a band name for Fleetwood and the McVies; it was the core of their identity. Anyone familiar with the English court system would agree that things had changed little since Dickens wrote his epic legal satire, *Bleak House*, during the reign of Queen Victoria. Fleetwood Mac would be locked up in an expensive war of legal attrition for years.

American-born musician Bob Welch, who had recently joined the band as a cowriter and lead guitarist, called the other members from his home base of California. He knew a way out—the only way out, if they wanted to keep making a living: come to the United States. Their contract did not bar them from performing in America, and they could make a new life there while waiting for their previous one to be returned to them. With some misgivings and anticipatory pangs of homesickness, Mick, John, and Christine packed up and boarded a plane. They reasoned that they could always come home if they were unhappy, and they had nothing more to lose.

It was to be the best move they ever made. Nine months later, while shopping for groceries in an L.A. supermarket, Mick Fleetwood happened upon a friend who suggested Mick check out a studio called Sound City; the friend thought it would be perfect for Fleetwood Mac's album. It was at Sound City, that Mick first encountered a Californian folk-rock duo named Buckingham Nicks. Together they, with John and Christine McVie, would make rock music history, something neither band had been able to do on its own.

Two years after their chance encounter, (Welch had left the band and embarked upon a solo career), Mick Fleetwood, Stevie Nicks, Christine McVie, Lindsey Buckingham, and John McVie finally decided on a name for the album they had just completed. They went with bass player John McVie's suggestion of *Rumours*, in wry recognition of all the media gossip the new lineup had generated in their short two years together. Everybody had high expectations for the album, since its predecessor, the eponymous *Fleetwood Mac*, had astounded all those who had previously written off the band as a commercial also-ran. *Fleetwood Mac* had become Warner Brothers's best-selling album a year after its release. The "new look" Fleetwood Mac had created a sensation, and young women flocked to their concerts dressed like Stevie Nicks, in black chiffon and Gothic top hats.

Hype is a terrible thing; it inflates expectations and puts unreasonable pressure on all involved in creating a product. *Rumours* was a rare triumph, an album that met every expectation—of the record buyers, the critics, the retailers, and the record company itself. It also survived the corrosive effect that hype can have on a band's credibility. In the decades that followed its release, Rumours's legend has grown brighter, and it continues to sell; it is unquestionably the best-selling soft rock album of all time. Its timeless blend of pop, folk, and country has attracted fans of all genres of music, and the band's candid portrayal of the turmoil in their personal lives has won them loyal public affection.

Although Rumours was conceived at a time of great excess, when the musicians who made the music—and the companies who sold it—indulged in everything, at every opportunity, it was also a period of innocence, of good times. Rumours was made when the record companies were at their most affluent. Yet, as so many of those interviewed in the following pages will attest, this wealth was spread around. In addition, artists were given the time and freedom they needed to develop; there were long-term investments in careers. Most of all, music was the common language of youth culture. Those were the years before multimedia entertainment knocked rock music off its throne, before the record companies began their nervous budgeting and one-shot career strategizing. Rumours may be a platinum record, but it stills speaks of the golden California days before irony usurped innocence, and before punk rock came along and tried to make rock music feel old and stupid.

As a coda to the magnificent success of Rumours, Fleetwood Mac made an album whose adventurous, maverick content only served to emphasize the gilded triumph of its predecessor. Tusk was released just as the record business went into dramatic decline, and all who heard it realized it was not going to generate the kind of revenue needed to save the tottering industry. Although *Tusk*'s artistic value has now, finally, been acknowledged, it was considered by many commentators of its day to be a self-destructive move on the band's part. Lindsey Buckingham, its main instigator, was banished to the naughty corner, and the band's next studio album, *Mirage* was ... well, that's another story.

This is the tale of *Rumours*, an album made by a band that, at the height of its globe-spanning, multiplatinum-selling, gossip-ridden popularity, was managed by its drummer. A former grubby blues group reborn eight years later as soft rock gods. A band that, through many years of spirit-sapping setbacks, was held together by Mick Fleetwood (who, incidentally, rarely got a writing credit in the band's catalog of platinum songs). It is the story of the Fleetwood Mac lineup that gelled in early 1975—five relationship ninjas whose most painful and grueling personal agonies were recorded in the grooves of their platinum albums.

During the height of the cocaine-ridden years of hollow excess that mythically characterized the mid-to-late 1970s in the L.A.-based music industry, their personal struggles and heartaches—and the rumors that went with them—gave their music a beating heart and a compelling humanity. Hidden in the 11 songs that comprised the original release of *Rumours* are endless hours of crushingly awful times, made no less difficult for being shared among the five of them, and a mortification of the spirit that would make sleeping on a bed of nails look like a pajama party.

Peter Green's blues

England, 1968: A restless 21-year-old guitar prodigy and former apprentice butcher from London's East End, Peter Green (né Greenbaum) had just formed a band around his spookily inspired blues guitar playing. He named it Fleetwood Mac, in honor of his drummer, Mick Fleetwood, and John McVie, the bass player he hoped to entice into the band. British music had been smitten by a blues epidemic. It coursed the veins of the jazz clubs, pubs, and student union halls. Says Bob Brunning, Fleetwood Mac's first bass player, and author of *Fleetwood Mac: Behind the Masks*, "There were tons of local bands. Some broke through, the ones we all know today. Some made it to the States, like the Rolling Stones. It was a very healthy club scene—so many places to play, mostly back rooms of pubs—nobody had got to arenas at that stage." By 1967 clubs rang to the wailing of steel strings at the hands of Eric Clapton and U.S. import Jimi Hendrix, two new and revered masters of cool. According to British jazz singer and raconteur George Melly, the London area was so filled with the music of The Delta that it was playfully nicknamed the Thames Valley Cottonfields.

The blues—black American folk music originating in the Mississippi Delta of the United States—began crossing the Atlantic in the mid-1950s. The first blues record buyers tended to be a small, intellectual group of music listeners—

the same listeners who had encouraged the earlier traditional American jazz revival. American rock 'n' roll burst through with more commerciality around the same time, and many of England's future blues stars spent their youth listening to Chuck Berry and Little Richard. However, little was heard of these new American styles on the state-sanctioned BBC radio stations; Radio 1, the home of rock, pop, and soul music, would not be founded until 1967. It was left to the small British clubs and the American Forces Network, broadcasting from Frankfurt, Germany, to help propagate these rigorous and raw new sounds.

"For Peter Green, his greatest influence, without a doubt, is B. B. King," says Brunning, "and people like T-Bone Walker, who inspired B. B. King. He tried to adopt that style, in the sense that B. B. King is an exponent of making one note count where other people might play twenty." Green, a young master of the traditional Delta blues, could be as erratic in person as he was exceptional in his playing. Although Green could have easily been one of the great guitar heroes of the 1960s, alongside peers Jimmy Page and Eric Clapton, he had little interest in material fortune. His inner life dictated his path; a journey of increasing psychological turmoil and pain. He would soon be unable to sustain balance in his personal life, and his subsequent journey took him into some dark and strange corners. Much of this was witnessed by his close friend, Mick Fleetwood—a long, angular youth who had had his own share of troubles in his 17 years by the time he met Green. With Fleetwood and Green came a meeting of spirits, an understanding that went beyond the joy of jamming together.

Mick Fleetwood was a dreamer, an empathetic youth for whom music was as much about chemistry as it was about technique. He was born the second child of RAF wing commander Mike Fleetwood and his wife, Biddy. Although he was intelligent and inquisitive, he never excelled academically, in an era when there was no recognized alternative. He wound up dispirited by his experiences at school, but he did realize his talent for bringing people together— for communicating. He taught himself to play drums by playing along in his bedroom to Everly Brothers records and by mimicking the drumming of Tony Meehan from Cliff Richard's legendary backing twang band The Shadows.

However, Mick seemed in many ways to have been born into the wrong era. As the rest of the world became infatuated with The New, he excelled at fencing, a sport of old. He also found that he loved to perform in a theatrical setting, preferably dressed for a female role. When Mick dressed in women's clothing, be it at a high school play or on the cover of *Rolling Stone* 20 years later, he always gave the impression of being not so much an aspiring drag queen as a medieval mummer born out of time.

The Fleetwood family had a long tradition of serving their country in the armed forces, and in some ways this was to continue in Mick; nurturing team spirit and keeping the troops together were missions he would be called upon to perform over and over. Mick Fleetwood's compulsion to mediate would prove vital to keeping together the band personnel while recording *Rumours*. Without Fleetwood's dedication to the cause, the world may have ended up with several solo albums instead of their celebrated group effort.

The Fleetwood family were also lovers of the arts, and they defied the stereotypical representation of army folk as unyielding, regimented, and giving credence only to that which can be seen, heard, and ordered around. Mick's father, who wrote poetry, and mother recognized that their son was not cut out for the traditional post-public school careers in the white collar professions—or the army. Mick was deeply touched when his parents bought him a drum kit, and they gave their blessing for him to abandon school and head off to London, the swinging epicenter of popular culture at the time, in 1963 to pursue his dream of being a professional drummer.

To pay the bills, Fleetwood took what would be his one and only nonmusical job, a position in the accounts department at the upscale London department store, Liberty. He was hired, he recalled, because, although his maths skills were dismal, he was well-spoken. The 15-year-old Mick had a thoroughly wretched time there, and he struggled with his job of approving credit applications. Finding it impossible to keep up with the work, he sped things up by approving *all* applicants. It didn't take him long to realize that his destiny lay elsewhere.

After a foray with a group called the Senders, he joined his first major band, a bunch of swinging Londoners who called themselves the Cheynes. The band swung fearlessly with the cream of the scene, from the Spencer Davis Group, to the Animals, to the legendary John Mayall & the Bluesbreakers. When the Cheynes split, Mick joined the Bo Street Runners, a band best known for winning a competition organized by the swingingest mod-music TV show of the day, *Ready Steady Go!* During this time, he fell in love with a young model named Jenny Boyd. Jenny's sister, the equally photogenic Patti Boyd, was well known as one of London's most famous models and the girlfriend of Beatle George Harrison. The courtship of Mick and Jenny was one of hesitant devotion; Fleetwood has always pronounced himself a little insecure when wooing the ladies—although a blunt observer might note that he has done very well for himself over the years.

Fleetwood met Peter Green when he joined his next band, Peter B's Looners, which was led by an old friend of Mick, keyboard player Peter Bardens. Peter B's Looners then changed their name to Shotgun Express and added a new vocalist, Rod Stewart, who was then a rising star in the U.K. blues scene. Fleetwood and Green roomed together during band tours, and during this time they developed a deep artistic appreciation of each other. It was a friendship of opposites, and an association that would continue through difficult times.

Green taught Fleetwood leadership by example. He was a patient man with an endless love of music, and Fleetwood appreciated how Green would take time to help his band members when they were struggling. Fleetwood recalled a moment during the early years of Fleetwood Mac, when Peter Green led the group. The drummer remembered being beset by a bout of rhythmic dyslexia during a live show, which caused him to panic. Many virtuoso bandleaders would have glared and even fired him for incompetency. Peter Green, Fleetwood recalled, came over and patiently guided him with his own hand, helping him lock into the rhythm. Long after Peter Green had left the band, Mick Fleetwood maintained a passionate loyalty to the band, which he saw as his friend's legacy. In later situations of conflict that might have resulted in many other bands breaking up, Fleetwood would go into mediation overdrive, passionately determined to keep the band together. And he succeeded. When Fleetwood Mac faced its greatest test of unity, during the recording of *Rumours*, Fleetwood and the other band members were able to draw on past struggles and derive enough emotional strength to actually complete the recording and promote the record, while the press took bets on how long the band would stay together.

Green also taught Fleetwood to have a very fussy ear when it came to guitarists. This skill, combined with Fleetwood's natural intuitive ability to sense when a player was capable of musical magic, gave the drummer the gift of foresight. In late 1974 he heard Lindsey Buckingham playing guitar, and he knew immediately that he had to act to secure his services. He did so, and less than a year later, Fleetwood Mac had made an album so successful that it surprised even the band's own fans.

During that U.K. blues explosion, Peter Green had become a good enough guitar player to warrant an invitation to leave Shotgun Express and to join John Mayall & the Bluesbreakers as a temporary stand-in for new blues superstar Eric Clapton when the guitarist who would become known as "God" took a sabbatical. The Bluesbreakers functioned as a kind of unofficial "blues farm" for raising young, hotshot musicians. As well as being an attraction in its own right, the band backed many of America's most celebrated blues heroes. Mayall's protégés included Eric Clapton, Mick Taylor (later of the Rolling Stones), Peter Green, and a bass player named John McVie. Green joined the Bluesbreakers on a permanent basis after Clapton made arrangements to form the torrid supergroup Cream.

In April 1967 Green encouraged his friend Mick Fleetwood to audition as the Bluesbreakers's new drummer. Fleetwood passed the test, and he found himself playing alongside John McVie, whom he had first met at an after-hours jazz and rhythm-and-blues club on Wardour Street, the Flamingo Club. McVie, an obstinate yet deeply sensitive soul, was born in 1945 to parents Reg and Dorothy. He too learned to play by listening to the Shadows' records, particularly to performances of its much-respected bass player, Jet Harris. After leaving school he joined the civil service, where he worked for the Inland Revenue, the government department responsible for all national taxation. Working for the Tax Man was not McVie's calling, and he soon hung up his button-down shirt and took up work as a professional musician. In April 1963 he joined the Bluesbreakers and earned a steady living playing music. Bob Brunning remembers that McVie's classic bass style was in evidence even in those early days. "McVie's playing was absolutely solid as a rock: unfussy, no frills, no solos, no Jaco Pastorius stuff."

Both McVie and Fleetwood had an uncluttered style. "Mick Fleetwood was very open to playing with different people," recalls Brunning, "as long as he didn't have to change his style. He was, and still is, a completely straightforward drummer, and it works with a lot of different styles. I don't s'pose he's played a [traditional] drum solo in his life!" While neither Fleetwood nor McVie was a virtuoso, their disciplined refusal to indulge in distracting busyness meant that they were able to give depth and support to the melodic components of the band. It is worth noting that the composition of the Bluesbreakers was similar to that of Fleetwood Mac during the making of *Rumours*. Many bands had a focal point, usually the vocalist. Both the Bluesbreakers and the *Rumours* incarnation of Fleetwood Mac had multiple key personalities. While this gave both bands variety and longevity, it meant that their rhythm sections needed to find a way to support the melodic players without stepping on them. Mick Fleetwood's and John McVie's stretch at Mayall's intense "Bluesbreakers University" left them with invaluable experience when it came time to integrate the multiple talents of Christine McVie, Lindsey Buckingham, and Stevie Nicks.

Fleetwood's time in the Bluesbreakers was quite short-lived; he was asked to leave after one too many drinking sessions with John McVie. (The latter had already been let go several times, but was always reinstated by Mayall.) Peter Green left the Bluesbreakers soon afterward; he was eager to stretch his musical talent and to see the world, especially the United States. He was persuaded to form a new band, one that was entirely his own, by a London-based blues enthusiast named Mike Vernon. Vernon was also an A & R man for the Decca U.K. record label. With his brother Richard, Mike Vernon set up an independent blues label named Blue Horizon, which eventually established a coveted national distribution deal with the mighty CBS. Says Bob Brunning, "Mike was the one saying to Peter, 'Get out of John Mayall and form your own band.' Mike originally wanted to get them on Decca—and Decca has made some spectacular mistakes, such as turning down the Beatles—they also turned down Fleetwood Mac. That's how Blue Horizon was born."

Peter Green brought in Mick Fleetwood to play drums, and he also hired a slide guitar player named Jeremy Spencer. Spencer was a lively character, an Elmore James fanatic given to performing lewd Elvis impersonations onstage while spending his offstage hours studying the Bible with his young wife—habits that just screamed "Fleetwood Mac guitarist." Green's master plan was almost derailed when his bassist of choice, John McVie, could not be persuaded to leave his steady paying job with Mayall. Confident that he would eventually get his way, Peter Green continued to call his band Fleetwood Mac, a name that had originated as a Bluesbreakers song title honoring the band's drummer and bass player.

In the meantime, Green, Fleetwood, and Spencer began auditioning for a temporary stand-in. Bob Brunning was one of the hopefuls who answered their anonymous ad and went over to Green's council flat in Putney, southwest London.

"I know one of the reasons I got the job was I'd hauled my bass amp up the stairs—we both had Vox amps. I had one with a whacking great 18-inch speaker and he had a tall one. I saw him looking at my amp, and I was looking at his 'cause it was taller and bigger; mine was smaller and more powerful and fatter sounding. Peter was a very blunt guy; he said, 'Bob, I don't half fancy your amp. Wanna swap?' and I said, 'Yeah, I like yours better than mine.' He used it for ages. Those big, powerful bass amps are great for guitar players because they've got more depth." At the time, Brunning was not terribly familiar with the blues, but he had heard of Peter

Green. "I said to him, 'What a good name you've got, 'cause it's the same as that bloke in John Mayall.'" Green quickly advised him he was that bloke. "Yes, Peter Green really did call me a bloody idiot—and he was absolutely right."

"When we'd bashed through [the audition] and he said, 'You'll do,' he goes, 'I must tell you, my biggest influence is B. B. King.' So I said, 'I've never heard of him,' and Peter practically passed out. 'Christ, what?!' I thought he was going to say, 'Leave the room,' but he just piled all these albums on me.

"Peter Green gave me an absolute crash course in the blues. He was a very good bass player. He also piled John McVie things at me and said, 'Listen, that's the way to do it.' It wasn't terribly hard, but it took a while. He was very patient; he didn't do so much teaching, as when we were warming up, he'd come over and say, 'Hey, why don't you try it like this?', and I had the sense to listen. Mainly he just thrust piles of records at me and said, 'Go listen.'"

The new quartet debuted in August 1967 at a dauntingly expansive and high-profile venue: the seventh annual Windsor Jazz and Blues Festival, which would later relocate and reemerge as the Reading Festival. Fleetwood Mac was at odds with much of the British blues world, tending toward old-fashioned Chicago-style blues instead of the more progressive acid blend of many other blues-rock bands. This allegiance to more streamlined stylings would leave the band well prepared when they emerged from their blues-rock chrysalis in 1975 and became a pop-rock band.

Eventually, McVie did join Peter Green's Fleetwood Mac. John Mayall had brought in a horn section to Bluesbreakers, which was encouraged to play in the newfangled and fashionable freeform style, something that horrified the purist bass player and prompted him to leave that band. Recalls Brunning, "John McVie wasn't an extreme purist as in drumming his feet and throwing his toys out of the pram, but he liked blues; he didn't want anything else. If bands did get a bit jazzy and horn influenced, he'd move on."

Bob Brunning had always known McVie would replace him, and he vacated the spot, taking with him some good memories and the same valuable lesson in musicianship that Fleetwood and McVie had learned. "Peter Green taught me what I've never forgotten: less is more. That's what I do to this very day—I play straight down the line, four to the bar. Fleetwood Mac was good fun. They were a bunch of mates making rude comments and telling filthy jokes—typical band members, really, really nice guys—although maybe Jeremy was a bit strange [laughs], but that's Jeremy, isn't it?"

Peter Green finally had his band. Brunning went on to join the Savoy Brown, which would later provide another incarnation of Fleetwood Mac, with another band member, Dave Walker, and a legendary road manager, John Courage. Mick Fleetwood and John McVie began what was to be many years of nonstop recording and touring. At the same time, another future Fleetwood Mac member, Christine Perfect, who would later become Christine McVie, was beginning a similar journey. By the time Fleetwood Mac was reborn with Buckingham and Nicks, Mick Fleetwood and the McVies would have eight solid years of road experience behind them, including much practice at swiftly integrating new band members—much more so than most "new" bands starting out. This work ethic and practiced adaptation would be a key factor in the band's breakthrough following the release of 1975's *Fleetwood Mac*, when they undertook the crucial tour that resulted in platinum sales of that album, which in turn resulted in the willingness of their record company to underwrite the lengthy recording of *Rumours*.

Peter Green's Fleetwood Mac, however, sounded nothing like the band that would record the sophisticated soft rock classic album of 1977. The band's first albums, like those of its peers, were quickly recorded representations of their live sets, which was just fine as far as the audience of the day was concerned. Led Zeppelin's breakthrough first album of 1969, wherein the blues was transformed into heavy metal, was recorded in a mere 36 hours, and that band went on to make four albums in two years, a pattern that was paralleled by Fleetwood Mac. The band's first album, entitled *Peter Green's Fleetwood Mac*, sold in sufficient quantities to chart, and in 1968, that incendiary summer of love and political unrest, Fleetwood Mac made its first trip to the land of its destiny, the United States of America, playing its first show there at San Francisco's Fillmore West. At that very time, a young San Francisco band named Fritz was just starting out. But it would be another five years before Mick Fleetwood would encounter Fritz's then-bass player Lindsey Buckingham and vocalist Stevie Nicks. Fate was not yet ready for them to meet.

Green and the others were wary about making the trip to the States, which was not an unusual attitude among the otherwise rough-and-tumble troubadours of the late 1960s. Bob Brunning explains that this fear originated in the perceived gun culture of the United States. "Then we were all terrified of guns—they were unknown in this country, apart from a tiny coterie of east London villains. In those days, us naive U.K. boys thought if you went to New York, you got shot. It was probably a media exaggeration."

The white British blues bands that did manage to overcome their trepidations and travel across the pond effectively sold Americans their own music—music that had, until then, been marginalized in that country. Fleetwood Mac and its brethren were widely credited with opening the door for the black blues musicians who inspired them—a door that would surely have otherwise remained closed for the duration of their lives. Says Bob Brunning, "The English invaders—the Stones, Savoy Brown, Fleetwood Mac, Ten Years After—largely without exception, would say to their large college audiences, 'You've got these guys in your own country and you're not supporting them, for god's sake!'"

Brunning remembers those days well. "The Stones always used to put a blues band on as support—B. B. King, John Lee Hooker. . . . I've talked to many a white [American] bloke of my age who said, 'If it wasn't for the English bands, I'd never have known.'" Although fewer U.S. bands devoted themselves to this music, two highly respected ensembles did help to kindle the flames of the blues revival: the Paul Butterfield Blues Band and Mike Bloomfield's (the) Blues Project.

American audiences could have been forgiven if they'd looked askance at the evangelists crossing the Atlantic to spread the American blues word, but instead they gave the Brits a generous welcome. Al Kooper was then a member of the Blues Project. "[The Brits were received] quite well," recalls Kooper. "The most influential British album was the Mayall-Clapton *Beano* album. We all marveled at Clapton's tone. Of course the Clapton-Beck Yardbirds albums were listened to, But Keith Relf's vocals were not up to the guitar playing. All the rest [of the British blues-rock bands] were welcomed and appreciated."

Indeed, in subsequent years, when British audiences grumbled as Fleetwood Mac's music changed and evolved, America was always there for them, its audiences eager and more open-minded. And when the band went into exile in the States in 1974, the memories of this welcome surely made the decision to move a much easier one.

The band returned home to record its second album, *Mr. Wonderful*, splurging on four whole days in the studio. By now, Peter Green had chosen to drop his name from the band's name and the album was released under the banner of Fleetwood Mac. Unbeknownst to them, another piece of the *Rumours* puzzle was placed before them in the form of Miss Christine Perfect, a guest musician on the album. Oddly enough, they had first met Christine, a vocalist and keyboard player with fellow British blues act Chicken Shack, during their debut at the Windsor Jazz and Blues festival.

Christine Perfect was born to Cyril and Beatrice Perfect in Birmingham, England. Cyril was first violinist with the Birmingham Symphony Orchestra, and Beatrice worked as, among other things, a psychic and a healer. Like most members of Fleetwood Mac, Christine grew up playing along to Everly Brothers records. While still a teenager, she formed a duo with a friend, hit the clubs, and was promptly told by Mum and Dad to come back home. After she finished school, she went on to study sculpture at art school, where she met a young Spencer Davis. They occasionally performed music together for pocket money on the streets of London, but Spencer soon connected with a 15-year-old blues prodigy named Stevie Winwood to form the Spencer Davis Group. Perfect decided she wanted to be in a band as well, and her familiarity with the classic American blues artists won her a place in Chicken Shack.

"Fleetwood Mac and Chicken Shack were signed at exactly the same time by Blue Horizon," says Brunning. "Peter Green was a bit jealous of [Chicken Shack guitarist] Stan Webb, or at least very curious to see what the competition was, since Peter didn't really know him at all. He would haul the band off and say, 'Let's go have a look at this Chicken Shack.' They'd play the same places as us, and were very good."

It may have been the Summer of Love and all things new and beautiful, but it was still unusual to have a female musician in a hard-driving blues band.[1] Perfect's trailblazing did not stop there; her self-titled solo album on Mike Vernon's Blue Horizon label, which she made after she left Chicken Shack in 1969, was heralded as one of the first soft rock albums ever made. Her warm and mellow treatment of blues standards strongly foreshadowed her later work on *Rumours*, and it impressed those who heard it. However,

---

[1] There were bands fronted by a female rock vocalist, most notably Big Brother & the Holding Company, which featured Janis Joplin. Then there were all-female bands, from the ghastly cult band the Shaggs to hard rock bands such as the U.S.'s Fanny and the Runaways—and let's not forget champion bass player and bandleader Suzi Quatro—but these bands were largely marketed as novelties, whereas Christine Perfect was quietly integrated within a regular band.

Perfect was way ahead of her time, and the album's arrival went largely unheralded. Her style was unique, and it was hard to trace her musical influences. Comments Brunning, "I'm not sure where she came from [musically]; she was an avid fan of a lot of female singers, but—and I think it's a compliment—Christine was Christine."

Grammy-nominated producer and engineer Michael Freeman, who has countless credits in the blues field, was then a teenager living in London, and very much a devotee of Peter Green's Fleetwood Mac and its label mate, Chicken Shack. "I can remember the first time I ever heard 'When the Train Comes Back' on the Chicken Shack debut album, this extraordinary voice was singing that wonderful song, and everybody went, 'Who is this woman?' It was so beautiful and even." Perfect and John McVie were already romantically involved at this point and they were married in the summer of 1968. They spent the beginning of their married lives apart, on tour with separate bands.

Not content with two guitarists, Green went on to hire a third, with the intention of widening the band's range of musical styles. The newcomer was Danny Kirwan, a sometimes withdrawn fellow from the south London neighborhood of Brixton. He was a fan of the styles of many guitarists, from that of the Shadows's Hank Marvin to that of the French gypsy guitar maestro Django Reinhardt.

Bob Brunning remembers Kirwan: "Danny was very jazz-influenced, mainly Django Reinhardt, of course, and he also used to throw in a lot of big band-y phrases. I think that's why it worked so very well with Peter and Danny; they brought something quite different into the partnership.

When they put it together, it worked. They were both very good technically, they did harmony things—and they rehearsed. It wasn't just 'what should we do on the night.' A lot was really worked out; for instance, they played in unison like the Allman Brothers. Kirwan came from a quite different direction."

Kirwan brought a strong thread of melodic lyricism to the band with his deeply evocative playing and his skillful use of tremolo. The soulful keening of Kirwan's playing on the band's next single, "Albatross," was a fine example. It's a beautiful mood piece, with strummed guitar chords evoking the ebb and flow of waves, the lead guitar soaring, hovering, and swooping. With Mick Fleetwood's gentle and muted accompaniment, performed on the tom-tom, and McVie's steady pulsing, the song became a crossover hit with main-stream audiences. (In fact, it would be a hit three times over the years.) "Albatross" marked the band's significant move towards the more creative world of soft rock. Long after Kirwan had left the band, this warm melodic feel, which so complemented the work of Christine McVie, became the band's signature style.

Although "Albatross" was a hit in Britain, it did not please some of the band's existing fans. It is well known that a hard-core British blues fan is faster to anger than a pit bull with a sore head, and there was much grumbling that Fleetwood Mac had lost its way as a blues-rock band. Bob Brunning recalls hearing from Green at this time: "They were pop stars after 'Albatross'; they were on *Top of the Pops*. I got a lovely postcard from Peter Green; when 'Albatross' was on top of the charts in the United Kindgom, they were stuck in some miserably cold American town. [It said] 'We're in this 'orrible, bloody place … Thanks for going out and buying all those copies of "Albatross"!'"

Apart from the weather, Fleetwood Mac found a warmer reception in America, where musical boundaries were not so fervently observed. On the notion that "Albatross" was deemed a sell-out by some people in the United Kingdom, Al Kooper comments, "That's hilarious. Can you imagine if they did 'Rhiannon' back then?"

On tour, they stopped off in Chicago to cut what was to be the last of their blues-rock albums at the studio of the soon-to-be-defunct Chess Records, a label renowned for releasing the work of American blues masters. By the time that *Blues Jam at Chess* was released, a year later, the band's relationship with Blue Horizon was over, and Fleetwood Mac had strengthened its ties to the manager who eventually caused them to take that great and fateful step of moving permanently to the United States.[2]

In the band's early days, Peter Green had struck up a management deal with a man named Clifford Davis (who had legally changed his last name, Adams, to avoid confusion with another Clifford Adams in the business). Davis was eager to move the band to a higher-profile record label, and he soon found an opportunity when the band's contract with Blue Horizon expired. The short-staffed label hadn't noticed that its contract with Fleetwood Mac was in need of renewal. "That was a horrible mistake [by the Vernons]," says Brunning, who has written at length about the band's early

---

[2] This album was divided into two releases for the United States, the first named *Blues Jam in Chicago* and the second, *Fleetwood Mac in Chicago*.

dealings with management. "The band all regretted it in the end, but it was out of their hands. Mike Vernon was the very opposite of the Clifford Davises of this world; he was in it because he just adored the music."

Davis signed the band to the Warner Brothers imprint, Reprise Records, where it would remain, for better and for worse, until the present day. Their next album, *Then Play On*, was a major success, and it marked a new approach to recording for the band. Instead of recording their live act with no technical mediation, the band laid down a series of mammoth jams, which were subsequently edited. The album also included one of the band's best-loved songs, Green's "Oh Well." This song, which is still a live favorite for the band, is a simple, jazzy, open blues riff and vocal, as rhythmic as it is lead-guitar heavy, and it has easily adapted itself to the different playing styles of the band's successive guitarists. Echoes of the song can even be heard in the band's 1975 recording, "World Turning."

As Mick Fleetwood would discover in later years, talent alone did not hold a band together. Whatever drove Green to create his magical music also drove him to seek out different spiritual experiences, including, by his own admission, brutal doses of LSD. Green became disheartened by the grind of the business and by the small compromises of self and music that had to be made in order to earn a living. He spent several weeks begging the others in the band to devote Fleetwood Mac to charity performances and to forego personal wealth. The band, although far from being gold-digging breadheads, nonetheless rejected this vision. Green's disdain for the merely material, however, would endure: in

1976 he burst into the office of his accountant, David Simmons, waving a gun. It wasn't the first time a musician had resorted to violent threats in a royalty dispute. But it had to be the first time a musician did so to demand that his royalties be terminated. For this, Green would be sentenced to two years of psychiatric treatment.

1970 was a rough year in rock music. The Beatles broke up, and two of music's brightest stars, Jimi Hendrix and Janis Joplin, died of drug overdoses. It was also the year that Mick Fleetwood became the band's new spiritual leader, when Peter Green announced that he was leaving the band, during a European tour. Fleetwood and the others were devastated by his departure; they hadn't just lost a brilliant guitarist, they had lost a charismatic leader. To Fleetwood's credit, he rose to the occasion. Although he couldn't persuade Green to stay, he managed to convince the others that it was worth carrying on. A horizonless tundra of ferment and torment lay ahead, and the band somewhat suspected this. They just didn't know how difficult it would be.

atlantic crossing

Around the turn of the decade, it became the thing to do for bands to commune in the countryside, under the same roof, to "get themselves together" and such. Fleetwood Mac found this a fine salve for their troubled minds in the months following the departure of Peter Green, and they repaired to a couple of converted kiln houses in southeast England. It was here that they recorded the aptly named *Kiln House*, which featured a guest appearance by Christine McVie, who sang and played but appeared uncredited for legal reasons. In the autumn of 1970 Clifford Davis and the band bought a sprawling and often chilly Victorian mansion in nearby Headley, Hampshire. It was known as Benifold, and the entire band moved in with their families. This semi-communal living, a kind of Fleetwood Mac condo arrangement, was most pleasing to the band's drummer, a social creature who prized community and communication.

The importance of the Benifold experience cannot be underestimated, for it laid deep foundations that helped to solidify and support the extended Fleetwood Mac family. It gave them a secure place in which to vent intimate feelings, and the bonds created by sharing a living space kept the band together when the individual egos may have strayed.

To replace Green, the band looked to Christine McVie. As a musician, she seemed suitably "Mac-like" and diffident when it came to making logical career decisions. She had already retired once, from Chicken Shack, to pal around with

Fleetwood Mac before staging a comeback in the form of her solo album on Blue Horizon. She then retired again—just as the album was released. Her reason, she claimed, was the "disastrous" live tour undertaken to promote this album. Christine embodied all of the qualities that the band valued: a great ear, fine musicianship, a warm heart, and a legacy of career chaos. In August 1970, two months after her second retirement at the creaky old age of 27, she made her second comeback, this time as a full-time member of Fleetwood Mac.

The band's lineup lasted six months, whereupon Mick was again required to mediate and motivate. They found themselves in San Francisco, beginning a three-month tour, when the San Fernando Valley earthquake hit southern California, their next stop. Jeremy Spencer refused to board the plane, convinced that Armageddon was upon them. A pep talk from Mick got him as far as Los Angeles, but that was the end of the line for Spencer. He walked out of the hotel and into the arms of a religious cult. He never came back. Clifford Davis saved the band from financial catastrophe by begging Peter Green to come to their rescue, which he did, canceling his scheduled gig as a farmhand and joining them on tour. After this bittersweet reunion, the band was forced to rebuild itself for the second time in 18 months.

An old friend of the band from San Francisco, Judy Wong, introduced the Fleetwood Mac to its next member, a guitarist who would provide significant support and energy when they needed it most. He would also give their songwriting new direction. Bob Welch was a veteran of several U.S. rhythm and blues groups, including an outfit called the Seven Souls, which also included two future members of Rufus.

Welch's deep interest in jazz had prompted him to move to Paris, where this music enjoyed popular support. It was here that Judy Wong found him, running down his bank account. She persuaded him to use the last of his money to buy a ticket to the United Kingdom in order to meet Mick and the Benifold crew. Although he was clearly an accomplished writer and musician, it was the chemistry between the band members that got guitarist Bob Welch the job in April 1971.

He made quite an impression on Michael Freeman. "I liked Bob Welch. I used to run a magazine called *Stage Pass*, in Chicago, and interviewed him when he had [mid-1970s band] Paris. He was a very, very interesting guy. He was a little flamboyant; when you're sitting talking to a beret'd Bob Welch with huge glasses and tons and tons of energy, [Fleetwood and the McVies] seemed much more reserved. It must have been a different dynamic," he chuckled. Bob Welch (like Lindsey Buckingham, who would eventually replace him) lived in thrall to a restless muse. His was a passionately cerebral approach to his art, and he was rarely satisfied with staying in one musical place, but was driven by the need to make new statements.

The first Fleetwood Mac album on which Bob Welch played, *Future Games*, was released in the autumn of 1971. It marked a significant turning point for the band. Welch opened the band up to new genres—a little jazz, a little funk, and, most notably, country rock, which would eventually be a key part of Fleetwood Mac's sound. *Future Games* enhanced the band's reputation on the underground live circuit in the United States, where their diligent touring regularly generated six-figure revenue.

Their next album, 1972's *Bare Trees*[3], found Danny Kirwan the dominant musical figure, writing five of the songs. It did as well as *Future Games* in the States, but merited a predictable "hated it!" from the U.K. blues fans. As the band dutifully toured these albums, more trauma came their way.

The first instance was the growing marital disharmony between the two McVies. Both have agreed that the pressure-cooker environment of life on the road, where they were in each other's constant company, together with John McVie's personality shifts after drinking, made life almost intolerable for Christine. She announced that she had to leave. Mick Fleetwood persuaded her to think of the band and to stay.

Taking on the responsibility of keeping a band together is like appointing yourself plate spinner of the universe at large; just when you think you have all of the elements whirling nicely, out of the corner of your eye you see the one at the end start to wobble. Danny Kirwan was definitely wobbling. By August, Mick Fleetwood claimed to be the only person in the band who could get along with Kirwan.

Since the group was traveling in two station wagons, a sense of camaraderie was vital—Fleetwood's value of band chemistry didn't spring from some swinging hippie ideal; it was a very practical consideration. Fleetwood's memoirs vividly describe a minefield of communication, and of Kirwan's self-destructive implosion and subsequent refusal to go onstage one night. Bleeding from a self-inflicted head

---

[3] Notable for containing two Mac classics—the melancholy pre-*Rumours* blues pop of Christine's "Spare Me a Little of Your Love" and the first version of Welch's "Sentimental Lady," which was to be a solo hit single for him later in the decade.

wound, he heckled the struggling band from the mixing desk. For once, instead of trying to talk the awkward band member into staying, Mick Fleetwood fired him, a painful but necessary task. It would be good practice for the future, when Fleetwood took on broader managerial duties that required a thicker skin. It was a matter of great sadness for the band that Kirwan, despite an attempt to lead his own band under the care of Clifford Davis, went on to live a troubled life in the shelter of psychiatric institutions.

For the third time, a Fleetwood Mac guitarist had fallen prey to a troubled mind. Could things get any worse? Legend has it that *Rumours* was the product of a unique rock nightmare, but clearly, as the band's history shows, it would be just the latest in a string of hypertensive marathons.

The band looked around for reinforcements. At Davis's suggestion, they added Dave Walker, from Savoy Brown, as lead singer, and Bob Weston, from Long John Baldry's band, on slide guitar, in the hopes of boosting their profile on the lucrative U.S. college blues 'n' boogie circuit. "Dave Walker definitely came from the Land of Rock," says Bob Brunning. "Savoy Brown were always much rockier, boogier, a more 'in your face' band. Dave brought that very strong front-man style; he'd work the crowd. Some lineups of Fleetwood Mac," chuckled Brunning, "couldn't give a toss about the crowd."

They also picked up road manager John Courage from Savoy Brown. Courage is quite a legend on the live rock circuit. A fiercely protective and hardworking member of the team, he was the very antithesis of some rather grand American roadies who would refuse to stoop to lift the equipment they tended. He, too, moved into Benifold.

With the recording of 1973's *Penguin*[4], the band seemed to lose musical momentum. It was no surprise that the critics at home wrote them off as a rapidly losing cause, and although the American audiences remained loyal, the inner chemistry of the newly arranged six-piece band was fractured; a ghostly guest appearance by Peter Green only added to the album's incongruity. Despite being talented in his given field, Dave Walker was not the right choice for the band. To further complicate matters, "Albatross" made its second appearance in the U.K. pop charts and viewers of *Top of the Pops* were told by the presenter that Peter Green had left the band (newsflash!) and that Fleetwood Mac had subsequently disbanded. This show was the one mainstream TV outlet for pop music in the United Kingdom, and millions of British listeners were convinced that Fleetwood Mac was officially "back catalog."

Throughout their history, in moments when its own momentum seemed to have turned on it, Fleetwood Mac has always managed to effect a change that takes it onto a new and brighter path. In 1973 Fleetwood and the other members readjusted the band's chemistry. Dave Walker was asked to leave the band—a painful event for John McVie, as he and Walker had spent many a happy evening together down at their local pub, The Wheatsheaf. Walker was a fine live performer and a focal point, but this was not a band that wanted one person to lead the show. In an online interview with the online Fleetwood Mac resource *The Penguin*, Walker

---

[4] Penguin imagery is notably featured on the album covers, business entities, and fan paraphernalia of mid-period Fleetwood Mac. It is not an homage to a rather odd album, but a tribute to the noble obsession of John McVie—he became bewitched by the creatures while living close to London Zoo.

himself commented that his role in the band was not defined, and that he was not able to be part of the creative process. This, coupled with some difficulties he was having in his personal life, lead to the parting. Walker remained on friendly terms with the band, despite his disappointment.

Walker's difficulty in being assimilated would contrast sharply with the experience of Stevie Nicks when she and Buckingham joined two years later. Because she didn't play an instrument onstage and was thus free to move around, she was effectively, the band's front man; however, her central role in songwriting, and her natural musical affinity with the two other vocalists and writers, resulted in Nicks's seamless blending with the band as a whole.

Mystery to Me, the album the band went on to complete without Walker, marked the last stage of their transition from odd blues band to soulful FM masters, and it was their second venture with coproducer, Martin Birch.

It was a popular album, and in it, Welch's contributions resonate more clearly. He has described the recording of this collection as being a mellow, warm experience, and it shows, especially in the spacy, jazzy live favorite, "Hypnotized." The song was originally written as a fast-paced blues belter so as to best fit Walker's vocal style, but after his departure Welch and Christine McVie retailored the song into a summery shimmer overlaid on a blues jam. It was a contemporary, radio-friendly song that would point the way toward Welch's deserved solo success and would affirm Fleetwood Mac's rebirth as a more pop-oriented band.

Welch's sophisticated vocal arrangements added new dimensions to the band's old blues tradition, and he also brought along some of the rhythm-and-blues shadings from his Seven Souls days. These blended in beautifully, and served as a precursor to the more deliberate spacing in the sound of the Fleetwood-McVie rhythm sections from 1975 on.

Christine McVie was not so well represented; it's possible that the disruption caused by Walker's removal and the scramble to fill the space did not serve her well. Her songs on the album are a handful of easy-rocking blues and her trademarked plaintive rhythm-and-blues odes. The closing song, the chronically despairing "Why," is a rare glimpse of her deeper self, and it illustrates why she inspires affection in so many. As on *Rumours's* "Songbird," her sentiments are sincere and simple, free of formulaic pop metaphors. At times like this, her candid, approachable alto seems to warm the space between her and the listener.

It was Bob Weston's suggestion to drop an original song, "Good Things," from the final album listing in favor of a cover of the Yardbirds' "For Your Love." This was recorded at the Record Plant in Los Angeles by Bob Hughes, who would go on to engineer the band's next album. Also present at the L.A. Record Plant session was an engineer named Cris Morris, who would act as assistant engineer throughout the recording of *Rumours*.

After the various sloughs of despond marked by *Bare Trees* and *Penguin*, the band was ready for more upbeat days. They took off to tour the States and were very well received. Unfortunately, as always seemed to be the case, the band found itself in jeopardy yet again when, during the tour, Mick Fleetwood said he found out that his wife was having an affair with his friend and bandmate, Bob Weston. This time, the person Mick talked into staying with the band was himself, and he chided himself for having long neglected his wife and child. It was not a fun time, but the show went on for a short while, as did the alleged affair. Fleetwood's resolve finally broke in October 1973. The band made it as far as Lincoln, Nebraska, whereupon Weston was "asked" to leave and Fleetwood told the band that he would have to take a break in order to recover his equilibrium.

Bob Welch broke the news to Clifford Davis back in London and he went on to oversee the band's subsequent legal battle with Davis. The manager was outraged when he heard the news, despite Welch's assurances that they would go right back to fulfilling their obligations after taking a much-needed break. In a series of phone calls and exchanges of lawyers' letters, Davis told the band he owned the name "Fleetwood Mac"; if they wanted in, they would do as he said. Mick Fleetwood was in no shape to carry on, however, and, after returning to England, he decided to take a trip to Zambia to clear his mind and regenerate his spirit. Christine McVie, who was always close to her family in the United Kingdom, went with him as far as England, while her husband repaired to Hawaii; the tension between the McVies remained a constant source of pain and conflict. Welch, who had gone to Los Angeles, remained there to deal with the legal mess and try to work out a future for the band.

The band was taken aback by the strength of Davis's determination. Bob Brunning interviewed Clifford Davis at length on this subject and found another side to the story. "Managers are the same the world over, they see a product," says Brunning. "I think Clifford genuinely felt he owned the product called Fleetwood Mac; it didn't matter who was on the stage, as long as they played the same songs and were called Fleetwood Mac. But us musicians don't see it like that, and a lot of fans, too! I do think he was genuinely bemused that anyone would object that he'd just put a [different] band together and called them Fleetwood Mac."

The experience led directly to the decision by Fleetwood and the others to manage their band themselves over the next few years—years of great success and equally great fragility. Treating the band as product would have killed the magic, and probably the act itself; the product could not be separated from the relationships that defined it. Indeed, the *Rumours* product *was* relationships, and needed to be free to take its own path—something few business managers would have been able to grasp.

The "fake Fleetwood Mac" tour fell to pieces. As the last gig crumbled, press reports described Davis's attempt to allay the audience's concerns with an onstage announcement. As he dodged improvised missiles, he assured the audience that they had not been given a fake band by proclaiming, "I AM Fleetwood Mac!" Says Brunning, "I believe [the whole situation] was a genuine misunderstanding and that [Clifford] genuinely felt that he was cheated. As for the band, they always supported each other when they were in trouble. Mick was like their brother; they all rallied 'round, even though sometimes they fought like cats and dogs."

Clifford Davis was a colorful character, and was himself an occasional performer with the odd writing credit on early Fleetwood Mac albums. Back in 1969, when he and the band were still on the same side, a few songs of Clifford singing over some Fleetwood Mac backing tracks were cut. These were later released as singles, but nothing came of them. After his split with Fleetwood Mac, he put together a band using some of the "fake Fleetwood Mac" members, and under the name Stretch, they recorded a song Davis had just written, "Why Did You Do It?" Davis said he wrote the song for Mick Fleetwood.

By February 1974 the band was at an all-time low. As if the Davis affair wasn't enough, legendary hotel-room wreckers Led Zeppelin, who had been banned from many high-end lodgings, began checking into hotels under the name of—you guessed it—"Fleetwood Mac." Nevertheless, Welch persuaded the group to relocate to Los Angeles in late April 1974, where they were forced to court anew their record label, Reprise Records. According to Fleetwood, the group left Benifold, their country home, with $7,500 and no equipment, their reputation in tatters. Live promoters were rightly suspicious of their authenticity, and the record company was very wary of doing business with a band that was in litigation with a determined English management company. Again, new direction and energy came—this time in the form of a music-business lawyer named Mickey Shapiro, who first met the band in summer of that year. Says Shapiro, "I had represented Bob Welch years before, in the Seven Souls. Judy Wong, who was the secretary of Fleetwood Mac at the time, had also been the secretary of the manager of the Seven Souls. It was like an old friend calling, saying, 'They've just come to America, would you meet with them?'"

The band met with Shapiro at his house in Los Angeles and Shapiro recalls a rather odd occurrence: Welch,

Fleetwood, and the McVies all separately told him that Welch might not be long for the group, and each person instructed him not to tell the other party yet. "It was rather uncomfortable. Each told me their story in different rooms of the house. It was very odd."

Welch had had enough of taking care of the band's business, and Shapiro became the interface between John's and Mick's new management company and the music business. With Shapiro's help, Reprise Records was finally convinced to finance a new album by the band. In theory it should have been an easy decision to make; the band sold several thousand albums every time it released a product, regardless of its lineup and circumstances. (Maybe Clifford had been on to something after all!) Any album by the band would certainly break even. The record company just needed to be told so.

As Shapiro explained to Mick Fleetwood and the band, Fleetwood Mac was at the wrong end of a "perceived value situation." The band always made money, yet it was not viewed as a moneymaking entity. Reprise Records made the band take all legal responsibility for the album's release, just in case Clifford Davis won the right to their name. Up the proverbial creek and with this contract as their only paddle, the band signed on and bravely moved forward into their new future.

Their first recording made entirely in the United States, this time with Bob Hughes at Angel City recording studio, was quite a musical adventure for the newly reduced four-piece group. A blues thread still runs through *Heroes Are Hard to Find*, and the live approach is still there, the club din of ride-and-crash cymbals, swampy blues guitars, and unfussy vocals always sitting back in the mix. With this album, however, the band's style expanded, with perhaps a little too much overconsidered variety. Bob Welch, like Lindsey Buckingham, his successor in the band, admired Brian Wilson and the Beach Boys. This is apparent when both Welch and Buckingham produce vocal harmonies. However, on this album, Welch's Beach Boys tribute, "She's Changing Me," is just that—a reproduction, rather than the integration of Wilson's influence which Lindsey Buckingham incorporated into *Rumours*. However, there are many moments of gritty loveliness from Welch here: vocal doodlings, hovering keyboard motifs, and hazy verses that give way to more driving down-home melodic bridges and choruses. All of this expanded the boundaries of the band and set a precedent for its future arrangements on both *Rumours* ("Oh Daddy") and *Tusk* ("Brown Eyes").

The album also features Christine McVie in much stronger form; *Heroes* contains one of the band's best pop songs ever, her easy, soulful "Prove Your Love." As usual, her songs have a traditional blues-rock format, but she weaves through this a top line that is both fresh and addictive, adding warmth and melody to the collection as a whole. As if to show she wasn't going soft, she also penned the album's romping, pounding "Bad Loser," allegedly a song about ex-manager Clifford Davis.

As a whole, the album has some fine songs, but there is a little too much diversity for it to have a strong identity. The departure of second guitarist Weston had left Welch with more influence as the sole guitarist. Again, the balance of the personnel had been adjusted. Bob Weston may not have had time to add any recognizable musical style to the ensemble when he was with Fleetwood Mac, but in the band where chemistry is king, he had had some kind of neutralizing effect. It was to be Welch's last album with the band. Had he stayed, the band might have struggled to blend his and Christine's styles. Admittedly, the two had a meeting point, as they showed in their joint arrangement of "Hypnotized," and in the album's utterly gorgeous semi-instrumental closer, "Safe Harbor," another "Albatross" throwback, but this time with more updated atmospherics and a lovely healing vocal coda. This composition by Welch was a fine piece of music with which to leave the band.

Fleetwood Mac had always been popular in the United States and had begun to incorporate more mainstream musical elements at the same time that the previously underground FM radio stations (that had supported their ragged blues days) went mainstream. When *Heroes* came out, early-FM-radio devotees were already complaining that their counterculture stations were being coopted by the commercial mainstream.

Still fighting for their band name, they took to the road, now playing to smaller crowds for less money at the hands of edgy promoters. The plan was to then take a break, rehearse some new material, and go into the studio for their third album in 18 months. In November 1974, Fleetwood began looking for a new studio and a new producer for their next album, before resuming the tour. In the back of his mind was the thought that the band was about to lose its fifth guitar player in almost as many years.

frozen love

Aaron Jess Nicks was a country singer who never made it to the big time himself. Mick Fleetwood has noted that A.J. was known for being "a bit eccentric," so it is not surprising that he would have a place, however indirect, in the Fleetwood Mac family tree. A.J. spent most of his life living in a makeshift home in the Arizona hills and performing at insalubrious bars. His son, Jess, as often happens, took the path farthest from that of his father and became a commercially successful corporate executive who moved his family from state to state, eventually settling in the the El Camino neighborhood of San Francisco. This was to be the rock 'n' roll playground of his teenage daughter, Stephanie "Stevie" Nicks, and her younger brother Chris. It was here that Stevie would begin playing acoustic guitar in the city's coffeehouses, and where she would eventually encounter one of her key musical inspirations, that legend of the blues-rock vocals, Janis Joplin.

But before Janis, there was A.J., her beloved, cranky Granddad. Stevie was born in Phoenix, Arizona on May 26, 1948, and it is here that she spent many happy hours with A.J., who taught her to harmonize with him in old-time country duets, and who encouraged her to practice playing the guitar by bribing her with pocket change. Could the temptations of rock 'n' roll be far off? She sometimes even appeared with A.J. at his shows, singing along and dancing on tabletops. Such was her popularity that A.J. hit upon the idea of taking the barely kindergarten-age Stevie on tour with him, an idea that was promptly squashed by Jess and mom, Barbara. A.J. stomped off into the night and was not heard from for a good two years, but he had already introduced Stevie to the energizing rush of connecting with an audience, and she would eventually follow him into the shadows of parental disapproval, dropping out of San José State University to realize her dream of artistry.

While in her freshman year at a high school in Los Angeles, Nicks sang with a Mamas-and-the-Papas-style vocal group called the Changing Times. She had grown up singing along to the Everly Brothers, and later, to the girl groups of the Motown era. Her first professional gig was with a Bay Area band named Fritz, which she joined in 1967, replacing their original singer. Playing guitar in this new band was Lindsey Buckingham, an acquaintance from her high school. Buckingham was one year her junior.

Lindsey Buckingham, the youngest of three boys, was born on October 3, 1949 to Morris and Rutheda Buckingham, a middle-class family living in the Lindenwood area of Palo Alto, California. Lindsey and his brother Greg were athletes, winners of swimming championships and widely believed to be destined for even greater things in the water. Lindsey, however, faced a forked path in the road to his destiny. One led to a shiny, happy varsity life of physical discipline and sure acclaim; the other began with the birthday gift of a guitar, and with the siren song of the transistor radio tuned to Wolfman Jack and other devilish DJs.

The latter path, assured his swimming coach, led to a life of moral decrepitude and deserved failure. Naturally, this was the path chosen by Buckingham. The teenager was intoxicated by the new, rebellious music coming over the airwaves, and by the sharp simplicity of Elvis's guitarist, Scotty Moore, which inspired him to practice intently. This was something he did very well. Buckingham never had trouble spending time with his music—his capacity for deep absorption in playing and in studio projects has won him as many detractors as admirers over the years. The freedom to do what he pleased in the studio has always been of central importance to him, and he would experience the making of *Rumours*, whose very essence concerned the relation of one to another, as a musical compromise.

Scotty Moore's fusion of driving blues and taut county picking influenced Buckingham's entire approach to the instrument. Buckingham developed a style that did not rely on the stern strike of pick against guitar string, which is traditionally used to hammer home rock 'n' roll chords and solo notes. Instead, he makes his stand with just his fingernails and flailing digits, a kind of rhythmic-folk flamenco. The approach brought him one step closer to his instrument, having cut out the "middle man" of a pick.

In 1966, Cal Roper, a Bay Area bass player, and his cousin, vocalist Jody Moreing, formed a loose-knit band that played folk songs and pop covers. They were soon joined by Buckingham, drummer Bob Aguirre, and another student from Menlo-Atherton High School, keyboard player Javier Pacheco. The band first rehearsed together in a warehouse belonging to Moreing's father. A few months later, Moreing and Roper left the band, which was moving in a more hard rock direction, and in came guitar player Brian Kane, followed soon after, in the summer of 1967, by a friend of

Aguirre's and an acquaintance of Buckingham's named Stevie Nicks. Buckingham switched to bass to accommodate Kane, and the new band, now known as the Fritz Rabyne Memorial Band (which would soon be shortened to Fritz) blossomed during the Summer of Love.

The band found itself at the epicenter of the global hippie revolution, where good vibrations and a liberated consciousness were the currency of choice. One of rock music's most significant events, the Monterey Pop Festival of 1968, which took place a mere hundred miles south of San Francisco, was effectively the commercial baptism of the northern California hair bands. Prior to this three-day festival of beads, caftans, and cash, local acts such as Moby Grape, the Steve Miller Blues Band, and Quicksilver Messenger Service had been ignored by the major labels. Now the labels were ready to sign anything that needed a haircut. It was an exciting time to be Fritz, an Anglo-Hispanic jam band with an eclectic set list and an increasingly enthusiastic local following.

Buckingham's parents were encouraging of his musical pursuits, and for the next two years Fritz rehearsed in the Buckinghams' garage. Eventually, under the care of dynamic local booking agent David Forest, they began to make enough money to afford their own practice space. Nicks's parents, however, were a little less thrilled about her interest in music, and they were surely even less happy when she discontinued her college studies around 1969.

Women were beginning to take a stronger lead in rock music, freeing themselves from the demure provinces of folk and pop after years of either strumming folk guitars or providing mere ornamentation. Nicks found role models in Grace Slick and Janis Joplin, ladies who took the raw immediacy and power of the blues and made it their own. Nicks's inner banshee began to stir. Standing in the wings of a Big Brother & the Holding Company show, in which Fritz had played a supporting slot, she saw Janis perform live, and her own future became clear. Joplin's ability to lose herself in the moment, to unleash every ounce of the power in her voice, to cast inhibition aside and to "get high on the sound" was just what the young poet Nicks wanted in her own work.

With Nicks fronting the band, Fritz became a popular act around town, and Stevie especially was singled out for notice. Onstage she wore skirts, boots, and shawls, keeping her look modest but funky. Unlike Joplin, she was never raunchy and lascivious, but she still had to contend with those who denied her artistic credibility simply because of her obvious sex appeal.

Fortunately, she continued to see herself as much a writer as a performer, and she soldiered on, working on her songwriting. Fritz would perform only two of her songs, which were described by former band member Javier Pacheco as countrylike and pleasingly unfussy in structure. Later down the line, her need for more musical space would be a factor in her pulling away from the band.

Fritz could rock hard, and Nicks's was not a voice used to fighting wailing guitars. The band did modify its set to include more laid-back numbers, which better framed her natural vocal talents, and, although her voice got stronger, Buckingham often took on the vocals of the heaviest tunes, affording the band a pleasing contrast and flexibility. Their three-and-four-part harmonies were a strong point, and Buckingham sometimes took the harmony pitched above that sung by Nicks; his distinctive, higher-pitched voice was also used in unison with the female singer, strengthening the vocal lines, maintaining contrast with the harmony sections, and generally adding an earthy weight to octaves that were unaccustomed to a male presence. Buckingham was an odd man-child guitar god who was meant to sing in a band with women. Nicks, in the meantime, also worked at onstage drama; to the chagrin of a couple of band members, she would perform Buffy Sainte-Marie's "Cod'ine" complete with simulated withdrawal throes and much angst. One wonders what they would have made of Nicks's later incarnation as Rhiannon, had she appeared back then.

1970 was the year that Janis and Jimi died, having fallen prey to the previous decade's rigorous excesses. The worsening mood of the band reflected this souring of the Good Vibe and divisiveness set in. Nicks and Buckingham were set apart from the others in that their songwriting was more personal than political. In addition, they were both keen to try their luck in Los Angeles, a desire encouraged by their booker, David Forest, who had relocated there himself. He had found a new management team for Fritz, which caused more conflict within the group; the others tended toward the very popular belief that Los Angeles was the home of all things plastic and phony. It was somewhat true; Los Angeles, in contrast to the Bay Area, was not a politicized city, but more a beast of commerce. This was interpreted by some San Franciscans to meaning Los Angeles lacked soul and authenticity, hence all the pop music and hits that originated there. Los Angeles had all the recording studios (chief engineer: the Man), but San Francisco had the live scene, the beating heart of rock, and the open mind, to say nothing of the third eye. Naturally, many L.A. residents disagreed, finding there an exciting element of decadence and freedom. It was a place where they felt unburdened by the reputation of righteousness that northern Californians felt obliged to uphold.

Accounts differ as to when Stevie Nicks and Lindsey Buckingham began their romantic relationship. In a 1992 interview with *BAM!* magazine, she stated that it was after the breakup of Fritz. If it was before the band's demise, as others have speculated, it was something they kept secret from the others in the band, for it would have been seen as a divisive special interest. Although they were not to live together until Fritz had split, it soon became clear to the others just where Buckingham and Nicks were headed.

In August 1970 Forest arranged for Fritz to record some demos with Keith Olsen, an L.A.-based engineer and former professional musician who was looking for young acts to develop. Three months later, Olsen went up to San Francisco to speak with the band, who was booked that night to play a Catholic high school dance. He found them in disarray, barely speaking and underrehearsed. The clean-cut high school seniors of 1967 had grown into hard-gigging longhairs, each with his or her own vision of how the band should be, with the exception of Buckingham and Nicks, who seemed to have a gift for staying in step with each other. Unlike the others, they seemed clear in their ambition to try their luck in Los Angeles, and Olsen encouraged them to move there.

Olsen worked as engineer at the L.A. studios Sound City, and he offered the penniless duo a great opportunity to get into a professional studio with a mentor and cheerleader. However, such opportunities in the music business always come with a tough decision to make for those who are emotionally engaged with their work. This would be no different. Olsen made them face up to the hard stuff: the first sacrifice to the god of rock was due.

"I was the guy who told them to bail on Fritz, telling them I wasn't interested in the other members," Olsen recalls. "'It's tough luck but ... you two have the talent—don't burden yourselves with the rest of them.' Sometimes it's cruel, very often it's cruel, but it's reality, and when—even back then—there are thousands and thousands of other bands vying to get the one, two, or three record contracts offered per year, the odds are hideous! The thing you need to do is really look to your strengths, look to where the weaknesses are, and eliminate the weaknesses. Yeah, it was pretty much my doing, and those guys didn't really like me that much for it, but I had to do it. They were all friends, they were still friends, so I'm breaking them up, that's hard to do."

Now billed as Buckingham Nicks, they moved to Los Angeles. Times were tough, and their families were not prepared to underwrite the risky business of rock 'n' roll. Nicks's folks withheld their support in the hopes that she would come to her senses and return to college. Instead, she earned money as a waitress (one restaurant made her dress as a 1920s flapper), while Lindsey held down a very occasional job as a phone salesman. But he came down with a debilitating bout of mononucleosis and returned home for months of recuperation.

Olsen offered the twosome money to help them out during the rough days in Los Angeles, but Nicks refused to take a handout and insisted on earning the cash, which she did by cleaning Olsen's Coldwater Canyon house. Buckingham inherited some unexpected funds from an aunt, and he used the windfall to purchase a precious four-track Ampex half-inch tape recorder, over which he slaved night and day, working on arrangements and becoming more and more accustomed to being a self-sufficient artist.

Keith Olsen is well known as a producer of some of rock music's best-selling artists. He has produced more than 80 artists and 210 albums, including such works as Pat Benatar's *Crimes of Passion*, Foreigner's *Double Vision*, and the Grateful Dead's *Terrapin Station* (total album sales amount to over 100 million dollars). A native of South Dakota, Olsen received his musical training in neighboring Minnesota and got his first pro gig touring as a bass player with country star Jimmie Rodgers on the hootenanny circuit. He eventually joined the band of Canadian singer and actress Gale Garnett. It was hard being a traditional folk band on a rock circuit and Olsen grew tired of playing the same 11 songs every night. He and some friends formed a band called the Music Machine, but a new path soon beckoned. Olsen happened upon a former University of Minnesota pal named Curt Boettcher, who was blessed with the good fortune of being able to go into a studio—anytime he wanted, and at no cost.

"I said, 'go into a *studio*?!' And so we started going in, cutting bands like the Association, and it was big fun." For the young musician, this was both a revelation and a chance to stretch. "From there, Curt and I got an independent staff producer job from Clive Davis at Columbia—CBS, at the time—in Los Angeles, where we spent the next year and a half. I think we were hired as the token hippies on the West Coast, because we were inventive."

Although rock 'n' roll was well into its teens, recordings were still very literal, with the sounds going straight to tape.

"[Curt and I] were not afraid of technology. If they didn't have a piece of gear or effect, I would go and build it, and bring it back the next day, with wires hanging all over it and batteries attached. We would make sounds happen, and that was out of the ordinary for CBS at the time, remember. Their biggest things were very 'if-it-happened-in-the studio-that's-the-way-it-was-period.' No other effects except for reverb. If you listen to Johnny Mathis, to Big Brother, Janis Joplin, it was what happened in the studio. Everything had to be originated by a human.

"We started becoming very inventive, in an era when that just wasn't done. From there, Curt and I and another guy from CBS formed a record company called Together Records—which was really untogether. We got to do some interesting projects; very few of them saw the light of day. It kept us going, kept us in the studio, and then, after doing my sixth project in a row with Curt, and all of them exactly the same, I went out on my own. I started signing bands to my own little production company. I signed Buckingham Nicks, [guitarist] Waddy Wachtel; I went out and got Stevie and Lindsey a record deal. I got Waddy one as well, and got another one for [bass player/singer] Jorge Calderon."

Olsen's discipline in the studio, and his ability to invent equipment on short notice, made Olsen the ideal engineer for the newly blended band that came together to record *Fleetwood Mac* after a mere ten days of rehearsal.

It was not enough for Olsen to be a creative and a technical talent; he had to complement these skills with a sound business sense, and he had to use all three to get a foothold in the Biz. "There was a guy there named Joe 'Jonas' Gottfried. He needed an engineer, really bad, who could bring in clients. I said OK, I think I can bring in some clients, give me a job. So he gave me a key to the studio and a by-the-hour job on clients I brought in. I barely made a living, *but*, I had a key to the studio and I could use it any time the studio was not busy. Sound City at the time wasn't a very popular studio, but out of that I was able to cut a demo with Stevie and Lindsey, with Waddy and Jorge. I brought in some acts, made a deal with Atlantic Records, wherein they could use the studio cheap, and Joe went for it.

"I brought in Dr. John, and I engineered the [Dixie Cups'] *Iko Iko* album, got very close to [head of Atlantic Records] Jerry Wexler. He really gave me a start, said, 'Come and spend some time with me in Florida,' and he talked to me for hours on end about the record industry. He was one of those guys, he did that for a lot of people. He got an awful lot of people into the music business who went on to create an awful lot of the records we've grown to know and love."

In Fritz, Nicks never lost the feeling of being swamped by the louder numbers. She craved a little more space to express her inner "Stevieness," and this new format gave her room to grow in her songwriting. The Fleetwood Mac bootleg trading world knows well a collection of Stevie Nicks demos, mainly comprised of guitar and vocals, which she supposedly recorded during the Fritz years, while the rest of the band played pool in another room. However, some former band members insist that this is not the case; it would seem that the songs date from 1972 to 1973.

Compositions such as "See the World Go By" and "Is There Anybody There" show Nicks's fondness for darkly minor folk melodies, pretty songs, and a little Mists-of-Avalon in the vocal vamping, performed while an acoustic guitar pedals dutifully in the background. Even these murky recordings show Stevie Nicks to have a vibrant vocal presence that is tuneful and robust, with a gentle prettiness to her timbre that would later be replaced by the rockier rasp that rendered "Rhiannon." The song "I Need You" is a pretty tune that demonstrates, rather spookily, how close Nicks came to following in the footsteps of Dolly Parton. In the songs, Nicks turns on a malty vibrato that is steady and strong. A.J. would have been proud. An arresting demo recording is "Cecilia," which is more sophisticated and features the multitracked harmonies of Nicks and Buckingham; in it, Nicks throws in a couple of crisp counterpoints, an otherworldly weave that was to be reprised in later years in the recording of "Dreams." The whole thing lays over a repetitive motif played on the low strings of a guitar with a Nicksily narcotic effect. It foreshadows the sound of things to come.

Says Olsen, "I brought them down to Los Angeles. They lived at my house, worked in the house, and in Sound City at night, after I worked, until we got enough songs for me to go out and make a deal—and then after they got their deal, they kept living at my house! And boy, what a huge budget that was, a total of the advance was $35,000 which included recording of *Buckingham Nicks*, the advance for the artists' signing, plus the producer's advance."

Listening to the songs of Buckingham Nicks today, in light of having heard Fleetwood Mac's mid-1970s sound, is spooky. Although as a whole, the songs and arrangements on *Buckingham Nicks* pale in comparison to the group efforts found on *Fleetwood Mac*, the vocal presentation—the textures, harmonies, and entwining of voices—and the folk touches and the occasional Grace Slick-isms are recognizable. They were Fleetwood Mac before they knew it. Their debut album hit the stores in September 1974 with an absolute minimum of promotional fanfare. At the ages of 25 and 24, respectively, Nicks and Buckingham went out on the road.

Buckingham, especially, remained on friendly terms with Fritz drummer Bob Aguirre, who played with them throughout the Buckingham Nicks years and went on to occasionally work with both performers in their solo recordings. Aguirre recalls Buckingham Nicks doing a showcase at a club called Art LaBoe's, on Sunset Boulevard, to which no one except their good pal, guitarist Waddy Wachtel, and a friend of his attended. A March 1974 *Billboard* review paints a picture of a duo with hesitant promise, fun to look at with distinctive vocal harmonies that work well with their country rock forays. The reviewer cited Buckingham for taking on too much with his lead vocal and lead guitar work. He also noted that, as a single instrument, Nicks's voice was a little abrasive when roaming the high notes, but that it was an exceptional instrument of harmony.

Reviews at the time, few though they were, were quite complimentary, but more than one made note that the album was doomed to promotional obscurity from day one, languishing in the barren hinterland of Polydor's marketing budget. The album contains many elements that would resurface on *Fleetwood Mac* and on *Rumours*—southern belter harmonies over fast-twisting, roots-rock guitar licks and wistful, stately tunes—the beaches of L.A. county meeting the folk harmonies born of Merrie Englande. And as in Buckingham's work with Fleetwood Mac, when he gets heavy, amid the grit and the shove there is still a lightness of touch, an airiness in the guitar solos that rests easy on the ear of the listener. The instrumental "Stephanie" is a plucked and courtly acoustic minuet and a direct ancestor of "Never Going Back Again." Buckingham's vocal sound is established here, and it features a distant folky texture that reveals a great debt to Cat Stevens. Stevie Nick's "Crystal" would be re-recorded for Fleetwood Mac's debut. On *Buckingham Nicks*, sung, as always, by Buckingham, it is the point where the act stands up and accounts for itself. It is a slow waltz in the heavy boots of a southern rocker, bluesy in the way of Little Feat, with a gospel feel to the vocal layering, and a soulful punctuation to the rich electric guitar. Buckingham's vocal here is softer and rounder, and is beautifully fluid and engagingly androgynous in many places—a quality that was to produce magical shadows in his later vocal work with Fleetwood Mac.

The later, raw sound of Fleetwood Mac is clearly recognizable, although it lacks the earthy grounding that Mick Fleetwood and the McVies would add. However, the songs are sometimes a little aimless in their melodic meanderings, reflecting the SoCal melodic lexicon of the times. The album's last song, "Frozen Love," is an exception; it's a complex, regal arrangement, the sound of Jefferson Airplane dancing 'round a maypole in 1537. The mournful melodic arc and the vocal arrangement come straight from the early English sacred tradition and provide clues to the origin of the arrangements on Rumours's "The Chain" and "Oh Daddy." It is complicated and intelligent in its progress, which steers clear of being progressive even as the guitar meanders and draws its themes in upside-down and twisty ways. The twin stars of the song are the deeply rewarding vocal exchanges between Buckingham and Nicks, and the simple purity of the acoustic guitar sound. It is little wonder that Keith Olsen would choose this track to demo the talents of himself and his studio to a prospective Sound City client—Mick Fleetwood.

As predicted by the reviewers, the album went unnoticed and unpurchased, and Buckingham Nicks was dropped by Polydor. This was another opportunity for Olsen to do for the San Francisco twosome what Jerry Wexler had done for him—extend a helping hand and show them the ropes.

"You have to, that's part of the deal you make, if you actually get to a point where you're making a living. Some of them say, 'Thanks a lot for all your help,' and others—well, look at it differently, and I'd rather not go into that. There are people who don't believe that collaboration is very cool, and I gotta tell ya, collaboration is an art form in itself; collaboration is how most music really is created.

"It strengthens the weaknesses, especially of people who choose their collaborators very carefully. Where you have a weakness—get somebody in there who isn't the weakness but is the strength. All of a sudden, you really do have strength in numbers, and can make it work."

This blending of entertainment-world egos is surely easier in theory than in practice. "That thing, did Van Gogh really let somebody else put a brushstroke on one of his works of art? That's the basic premise that every songwriter singer/artist, comes from; you have to break down that barrier first. Whoops! I'm teaching you how to produce records! With all that said and done, that's why most producers have horrible memories of working with bands, period. Because you have to do things where you put your own psyche in jeopardy because you know it's for the best, for the good of the project."

Olsen understood the duo's dejection, and he offered them some sorely needed cheerleading. "I can't say I was numb to it. All I said to them was, 'Well, you got to write some new songs. I'll make sure you get time in the studio, we'll demo them out, and let's find you another deal.' They started writing new songs—they were demoing them in the studio with their roommate Richard Dashut. He was taking them in the studio in the middle of the night—I was working another project—just demoing the material, a little bit here and a little bit there." Among these songs were tunes that would end up in millions of homes, such as "I Don't Want to Know." But, according to Bob Aguirre, these songs were turned down by every hit-hungry record company in Los Angeles.

Dashut had been introduced to Buckingham and Nicks while working at Sound City under Keith Olsen; he and Buckingham enjoyed an almost instant rapport. A couple of years younger than Buckingham, he was born in West

Hollywood in 1951. His college education would serve him well during the recording of *Rumours*; he attended the University of Nevada, Las Vegas where he studied philosophy and psychology before dropping out to return to Los Angeles, in the hopes of making music or movies. He began his career with an entry-level position—cleaning and polishing—at Crystal Sound studios, then was hired by Keith Olsen to work at Sound City. Buckingham's music buddies started dropping by the Nicks-Buckingham-Dashut apartment; Nicks would later tut-tut about those days, noting that she would come home, fatigued and downhearted after another day of dressing up as a 1920s flapper and waiting tables, only to trip over the likes of Warren Zevon, asleep on a floor carpeted with guitar leads and the debris of cheap escapism. This was not Nicks's scene.

After the nonevent that was their professional recording debut, Buckingham and Nicks were offered numerous opportunities to make a living playing music, but the invitations were to join cover bands and tribute groups, which, for the two passionate songwriters, was probably a fate worse than waitressing while dressed as a flapper. Zevon, a droll and abrasive singer-songwriter who was growing in notoriety, came to Buckingham's rescue by offering him the opportunity to make some money and not have his soul sucked out through his ears: the chance to play guitar and sing with one-half of Buckingham's boyhood heroes, the Everly Brothers. Phil Everly had left his brother Don for a solo career, and it was with Don that Buckingham and Zevon went on tour in 1974. Lindsey, who had been too-long sequestered on his living-room floor with a pair of headphones, was able to breathe some air into his work and to work on those shortcomings hinted at in *Billboard*'s live review.

With Buckingham on tour with Don Everly, Nicks was left alone in Colorado with Ginny, their poodle. She and Buckingham had been staying at a friend's house in Aspen, when Buckingham left to tour. Nicks was downhearted, deeply blue—and also deeply broke. Jess Nicks had been talking to his daughter about packing the whole thing in; he suggested she give the music business another six months, then she should go back to college. The clock was ticking. True to the Fleetwood Mac tradition, she pulled a bright treasure from the gloomy hand that fate had dealt her.

Penniless in Aspen, before her return to Los Angeles at the beginning of November, she wrote "Landslide," a future highlight of Fleetwood Mac's debut album and a song whose rich qualities have matured and deepened over the years. She considered her future with Buckingham, not just as boyfriend and girlfriend, but as creative partners who wanted a life that did not involve banging their heads against brick walls and living on ramen noodles—which is pretty much how Mick Fleetwood found them when he stopped by Sound City one day in November 1974.

ax heroes
are hard to find

Mick Fleetwood was not a man who would give up easily on his band. Bob Welch had finally shared his feelings with them, about seriously contemplating leaving Fleetwood Mac, and all signs indicated that they would soon lose another guitarist—this one a player who didn't just add to the band creatively, but who had also been active in the band's business affairs. Undeterred, Mick soldiered on.

He began scouting around for a studio in which to record the successor to *Heroes Are Hard to Find*. While out shopping with his children one November day in 1974, Mick happened upon an old pal who recommended that he check out a studio in Van Nuys called Sound City. Mick went with the flow and, with his kids and his groceries in tow, drove straight to the studio to meet Keith Olsen. While Mick's peas defrosted and his kids fidgeted, Olsen played him some selections from an album he had recently engineered and produced. The album was *Buckingham Nicks*.

"I played masters from the Buckingham Nicks album that I'd cut in that same room where Mick was sitting, on those same speakers that were up against the wall," says Olsen. "I turned it on and cranked it up and he was in awe; those records sounded really good for that period of time." Mick particularly liked "Frozen Love," the album's climactic guitar orchestra closer. Coincidentally, both Nicks and Buckingham were in the studio at the time, working on the follow-up to their unlauded debut. Fleetwood has mentioned catching sight of Nicks working that day, but Olsen recalls that they did not actually meet that day. Instead, Fleetwood made a mental note of Buckingham's guitar work and went on his way. In the meantime, Stevie Nicks, Lindsey Buckingham, and Richard Dashut carried on with their demos.

And so it came to pass that on New Year's Eve, 1974, there was more than the usual searching of soul and goal that comes at the year's end. For Nicks and Buckingham, it was a time of emotional self-questioning. Over in the Fleetwood-McVie camp, Bob Welch had confirmed that he couldn't take another step with Fleetwood Mac. Christine was now the band's only writer and vocalist, and Fleetwood Mac found itself again looking for a new blood. Fleetwood, realizing that the significant studio time he had already booked at Sound City was now somewhat useless, got in touch with Olsen.

"This story changes from person to person," says Olsen, "but this is the way it happened—there's been some selective amnesia going on here! On New Year's Eve, Mick Fleetwood gave me a call. He said, 'I've got good news and bad news,' and I said, 'Well, give me the bad news.' He said, 'Bob Welch just quit the band, so the project we're gonna start in February'—this was the one I was planning on living on in February—'probably won't start, because we don't have a guitar player.'"

Here was the economic food chain in action. The band had spent a considerable amount of time preparing their songs, and Olsen had already put in a good amount of his own time. "[This was] the project I spent so much time lobbying to make sure John and Christine wanted me to do the project with them, and we'd all agreed on everything." So much for the bad news—what good news could there possibly be? Olsen remembers how Fleetwood continued. "'But the good news is, remember those two kids, you played their songs for me? Do you think they'd want to join my band? We really only want the guitar player, but I guess they're a duo, aren't they?'

"And I said, 'Yeah, if you take one, you're gonna have to take the other, that's the honest-to-God truth.' So he says, 'Well, can you talk to them and see if they'd want to join my band?' So, I called Stevie and Lindsey. It was New Year's Eve. I had a date and a bottle of cheap champagne, and we went over. I sat upstairs with Lindsey and Stevie and my date, and we stayed there from 9:00 P.M. 'til 2:00 A.M., trying to convince them to at least try it."

It wasn't an instant decision. Joining Fleetwood Mac would mean that the couple would have to give up, for the time being, their dream of achieving success on their own terms, and would have to learn to live within the parameters of an already established band and its three bluesy Brits. However, there were definite advantages to the deal, not least of which was they would now be on a salary, a welcome change from their hand-to-mouth existence. Says Olsen, "I said, 'Why don't you give it the benefit of the doubt and at least try it for a few weeks, maybe a month? There's nothing to lose.' So they went and started doing rehearsals. They rehearsed and rehearsed, and they were salaried employees of Fleetwood Mac. They got in the studio, they signed a little deal with them, they hired me, they offered me a deal, I took it, and we proceeded, in 72 days, to record that entire album."

By the time Buckingham and Nicks joined forces with the three Brits, the latter had been through a fair number of dues-paying situations. They'd experienced the screaming girls, the 1960s blues explosion, and the whole swinging London extravaganza. The band had had a couple of comebacks and had gone through even more guitarists, each of whom had added crucially to the band's personality by also being key songwriters. Peter Green had shown astounding foresight in naming the band after its rhythm section, for they were to endure beyond the writers and virtuoso guitarists.

The band had been lucky to find a guitarist like Welch, who stepped up to the plate and provided leadership and business sense at a time when so many bands would have collapsed and gone their separate ways—and then they lost him, and had to start again. It is interesting to think that Fleetwood and the McVies—who, as a trio, would have been quite complete in most peoples' eyes—always seemed to feel that another player was required to fill out the band. They were a great rhythm section with a photogenic vocalist who was, moreover, a songwriter with a good pop ear and a high tolerance for uncomfortable touring. But the band believed they had to have a guitarist who would bring "something extra." Welch recalls that he did not have to leave the band, even when Buckingham and Nicks joined, but that he chose to do so, in order to seek new experiences. He recalls feeling that the band had run its course, despite John McVie's warning that leaving was the worst mistake he'd ever make. Had he stayed, however, the chemistry would have been vastly different, and it is doubtful that the band would have had enough creative room to make *Rumours*.

The two teams, the Brits and Buckingham Nicks, finally met in a restaurant. Nicks showed up in her flapper waitress uniform—a good match for Mick and his medieval costumery. Margaritas and good vibes flowed, and the deal was soon a done one. Nicks threw herself into her new association, running out to buy every single Fleetwood Mac album, looking for a common thread, a theme. To her credit, she didn't come up with the obvious "awkward guitar players," but with the quality of mysticism, something that ran through Peter Green's work, through Danny Kirwan's playing, and through the astral, lyrical speculations of the band during the Bob Welch years.

When the band finally all jammed together, they were thrilled, each in their own way, by the alchemy of their unlikely union. Christine McVie recalls getting chills when she, Nicks, and Buckingham first joined harmonies on the chorus of "Say You Love Me." Despite the spine shivers and the finger of destiny, Nicks continued to work another two weeks at her day job, dutifully playing out her notice. Perhaps she was also wondering if the new gig really would work out. She still had two months left on Dad's ultimatum.

One thing the new combo had was lots of songs. Buckingham and Nicks had a backlog of titles, and Christine had her own numbers ready to go. Buckingham claims it was easy to find the songs that would work with the new lineup. They also added one outsider song to their repertoire: the Curtis Brothers' "Blue Letter." They eventually settled on going forward with two songs written by Buckingham, four by Christine, and three by Nicks, as well as one rare collaboration, "World Turning."

The new band was in the studio for 72 days—they had come a long way from cranking out a whole album in one overnight session. They were not alone in this apparent indulgence. The rock world had moved on from the clinical sessions of the 1960s; now the studio vibe was king, and King Vibe often needed an awful lot of time to get things together. That a new band put together an album in 72 consecutive days—from its recording, mixing, and mastering to the all-important living-with-the-tracks time—was quite an achievement, especially taking into consideration the potential for power struggles in a band that had three songwriters and two managers.

"When you're prepared, it really isn't amazing," notes Olsen. "When you are not going in with just a wisp of one song idea and nothing else, 72 days of recording is really quite a lot. You can do miracles in 72 days—look at Nirvana's *Nevermind*. When you have musicianship, direction, good playing, groove, feel, and a vibe in the studio that's really good, it can get done in a reasonable amount of time and be really cool."

In March 1974 Nicks and Buckingham took time off to fulfill one last obligation as a duo—three shows in Alabama, where they enjoyed remarkable popularity. They had opened successfully there for a couple of bands and had benefited from a lot of local airplay. On the set list were favorites from their solo album, plus three of the songs they had recorded with their new employers. In Tuscaloosa they turned away 2,000 people at the door. In Birmingham, they were overrun back-stage by hundreds of well-wishers, who were astounded to hear that their favorites were about to join Fleetwood Mac.

Some interviews from the band have hinted at friction in the studio during the recording of *Fleetwood Mac*. Supposedly, it was not among the warring couples, as would happen during the recording of *Rumours*, but allegedly between John McVie, who was known to be set in his ways, and Lindsey Buckingham, who had become accustomed to calling all the shots in the studio. Olsen disagrees with these tales of ill will.

"Tension? No, not at all, the vibe in the studio was really cool. John walked up to me once, and in that amazing way that only John can, said [adopts the doleful and deadpan tones of John McVie] 'Excuse me, Keith, you know, but we used to be a blues band. I don't hear that much blues anymore, Keith.' What a perfect thing to say! And all I said was, 'John, we're doing pop rock, and it's a much faster way to the bank.' And he says, 'Well ...' and he turned and walked away, and everything was fine.

"That was the only thing that ever happened, during all those sessions, of any angst at all and that wasn't really angst, it was just an observation. Where you get angst is after the big hit—that's very common. It's common to question creativity, question songs: 'Are we copying some other band?' To question all these things, that just makes making records fun."

It makes listening fun, too. Compared to the previous albums of both parties, *Heroes ...* and *Buckingham Nicks*, this new, combined effort was a huge leap in aural sexiness. Buckingham Nicks had those great harmonies and a pleasing West Coast clarity, but in comparison to Fleetwood Mac, the duo's sound lacked body. The Brits certainly had a lot of power and body, but, in retrospect, their earlier albums lacked this new magical sound, these shimmering separate sounds, heavily layered yet retaining individual definition. No longer did Fleetwood's ride cymbal crash away in the background, sucking the air out of the vocal space. Now the vocals were higher up in the mix, with room to resonate. The drum sound was truly magnificent, the pounding tom-toms glutinous and immediate, showing off Fleetwood's impeccable timing and elegant simplicity. John McVie's rounded and assertive bass was given room to step out of the low-end murk and into the hooks of the songs. No more jamming; even the uptempo country rocker, "Blue Letter," was sharp and streamlined. In addition, the guitars, each with their own personality, were accorded the space they had long been denied.

The band chose to call their album *Fleetwood Mac*, an interesting and deliberate choice, especially for a band that had already been using that name for eight years and who had once released *Peter Green's Fleetwood Mac*. Mick Fleetwood wanted to make a deliberate statement, to introduce the new lineup, and, in a way, to chase away the ghosts of yesteryear. *Fleetwood Mac* also became affectionately known among the band's fans as the White Album—the *other* White Album, of course, since this unofficial title had also been used before.

Regardless of the name it was known by, the album was to be their most successful to date. It opens with the romping, rollicking "Monday Morning." The first thing the world hears of the new Fleetwood Mac is the slightly breathless, very distinctive folk-rock voice of Lindsey Buckingham, vivid and animated. All the instruments have their own space in the mix, with the drums being the superstars of the sound. Olsen reveals the secret of that sticky drum sound: "It was all about 'plastic puke.' First off, for the kick drum I had Mick use a real skin, not a plastic head. All the bass drum sounds had snap and crack and warmth, but the snare drum on the whole album was plastic puke. We put a piece up by the rim of the snare drum, then stuck a piece of tape across the back part of it. When Mick would hit the snare drum, the puke would lift up, and there'd be that bright, buzzing snare drum. Then it would flop down and would immediately stop the snare wire rattling, so it was a mechanical gate. We didn't have a piece of rubber; it would have been too easy just to get a piece of rubber. We had to, of course, go to the joke store." But could rock 'n' roll be ready for that revelation? "Oh, believe me, rock 'n' roll is—and was—ready for plastic puke."

The chorus of "Monday Morning" provides the public's first audience with the band's new harmony machine, a robust shower, underpinned by Fleetwood hitting some carefully rationed metal. Buckingham's song is followed by "Warm Ways," a "classic Christine" romantic ballad that serves as a beautiful meeting of the old and new Fleetwood Mac, and evokes memories of the days of Danny Kirwan and "Albatross" with its mellow, south-sea-island guitar motif.

While Mick was picking up a new guitarist and vocalist at Sound City, he also came across the song "Blue Letter" written by the Curtis Brothers, fellow Sound City clients and friends of Buckingham. It is Buckingham who takes lead vocal, with a little bit of California cowboy twang. Christine and Stevie are perfectly in step with some razor-sharp outlaw harmonies. Bob Welch has commented that Stevie Nicks adds a "wild and free vibe" to everything she sings, and this is a great example of that.

Track four has become so much more than a song to any fan of Fleetwood Mac, and certainly to its author, Stevie Nicks. "Rhiannon" was written around the same time as "Landslide" (track eight) and was first performed, much to Nicks's chagrin, in a fast-paced polka style, before this new Fleetwood Mac brought the song to its senses and closer to the writer's vision. The song was born of a name in a story she read in a paperback book, *Triad*, which she'd either picked up at an airport or off somebody's couch, depending on who's telling the story. The book describes the life of two women in modern-day Wales, and Nicks was captivated by the otherworldly archetype of Rhiannon, whom Nicks saw as a white witch. After writing the song, she discovered that there really was a legend of Rhiannon, and that the details in her song spookily echoed the myth.

Nicks often speaks of Rhiannon as if she were a voice inside herself, and she remembers being very perturbed when the song was later released as a single, fearing that the ancient goddess might suffer the indignity of not making the playlists and might end up in the cutout bins of America. Happily, "Rhiannon" rose up and triumphed, and gave the world a whole generation of female children of that name.

The legend says that Rhiannon had three birds, whose song could cure all pain. On the approach of Rhiannon and her birds, the sufferer would black out. On regaining consciousness, the sufferer would see the three birds flying away, hear their song, and realize that his or her pain was gone. The song is a dramatic example of Nicks's lyrical, rhythmic phrasing, simple and discreet, the syllables falling perfectly and evenly. The song is reminiscent of the shadowy nineteenth-century Romantic poets such as Christina Rossetti; it's a wedding of the unworldly and the flesh, mysterious steps in newly fallen snow. "Rhiannon" showcases many of the band's varied talents; the bass especially lifts the tune from that of a folk song to something new. Olsen recalls how the song was put together.

"They tried cutting that song on the first day of recording the track, and I think we did something like 20 takes. I kept this one take; I think it was take three or something. It had a feel to it, but they kept screwing it up. It was a complex bass line, a complex drum part, and it all had to groove to Lindsey's guitar, and it was something they were a little uncomfortable with. We came back a couple of days later and tried some more takes, and after about four hours of taking takes they went, 'Oh God, we're never going to get this track,' and they drove off. So I dug out that take number three, started editing together parts of it, borrowed another tape machine from another studio, made loops of the chorus and verse, two-inch tape loops—and started editing it together.

"There are about 17 cuts, and the only time you can really hear anything is at the end. Where it's fading out you will hear this one cymbal, every four bars, get clipped off, beat two of every four-bar phrase. The only place to cut this loop together was on beat two of the snare drum, and there was a crash cymbal that happened just before that point. And the crash cymbal goes psshhhhup—just goes away; I had to cut it off to make the groove work.

"We really didn't have much automation then. I couldn't quickly fade out the overheads every four bars. Going back into the verse from a chorus, it was easy to do because I could fade out the overheads; there were no cymbals in the verses. So, I cut this thing together, and they came in the next day. I said, 'Listen to this!' Lindsey had a big smile on his face; Stevie loved it, said, 'Hey, let's go!' That is the track that is on the record. That's also the track that gives Stevie fits; she injured her voice during the first tour by screaming that ending. She's learned not to do that anymore!"

At that time, making loops was much more challenging. Olsen says that "it wasn't really making loops. You were making a copy of a tape, and then splicing it and hoping that, when you overdubbed over the splices, the little scars would go away." Stevie Nicks would go on to write songs that were bigger hits, but "Rhiannon" established everything mystical and freespirited that she has projected ever since.

"Over My Head" has a rhythm-and-blues twist to it; a poppier take on Betty Wright's "Clean Up Woman" groove, with a disco dobro riff and Christine McVie's warm, curvy alto on lead vocal. Writer McVie phrases the lyrics deftly and easily, in a way that is very Christine Perfect. The backing vocals from Nicks and Buckingham hover distantly, much like the backups heard on old Persuasions and Delfonics recordings.

Says Olsen, "We all worked together on that track. Stevie and Lindsey were trying to fit into Christine's song, and so they worked together, trying to figure out the backing parts. We all sat in the control room for hours. Eventually we said, 'Wow, that worked good. Let's make it really silky.' So we'd double it and triple it and just make it silk."

One of the favorites from the Buckingham Nicks album is next on the album. It's a rerecording of Nicks's southern rock ballad, "Crystal." The time signature is slightly different here than in the Polydor original, but again Buckingham takes the lead vocal, and his androgynous tenor is pitched perfectly for the song.

It is followed, gloriously, incongruously, by Christine McVie's perky singalong boogie, "Say You Love Me." The song finishes with an infectious little coda, which is preceded by what sounds like a premeditated rhythm glitch.

"Lindsey's really good at that stuff," says Olsen. "If you listen, on "Rhiannon"—[sings the little pull-up that follows the first chorus]—he is such a musician. Being a self-taught guitar player, it comes from his heart, it comes from his soul. He doesn't know where it comes from; it's not one of those things where he says, 'Gee, I can go the six minor chord here to a five to a one.' He doesn't think of it theoretically. That's one of the things that separates Lindsey from everybody else. For instance, Steve Vai always knows the reason why he's playing something and why it sounds the way it does, because he's had so much technical training."

The band had rehearsed the song thoroughly, and the backing vocals, tight and lovingly structured, display this. "I thought that they blended really well, when doing backgrounds," comments Olsen. "Stevie had that shrillness; Christine had a warmth in her voice that wasn't there with Lindsey and Stevie, so it gave the vocal blend the added warmth that was necessary."

The second great song to emerge from Nicks's wood-shedding session at the electric piano in Aspen in late 1974 was the beautifully timeless and philosophical "Landslide." The words belie her youthful years as she meditates on the changes and the rhythms in life, and its fragility and beauty. Nicks had already been devastated by the recent death of her beloved grandfather, A.J. Then came an event that Nicks says changed her life forever. Her father had a very close call on the hospital operating table, and his family was sure they would lose him forever. These days, Nicks affectionately claims that everyone in her life thinks the song is about them, especially her father, Jess.

"World Turning" was, for this album, an unusually spontaneous song. It was written in the studio by Buckingham and Christine McVie, much to Nicks's admitted chagrin, for she and Buckingham had never collaborated as writers. The core of the song was actually an old Peter Green jam that the band would often use to warm up. The song became a great live favorite, and is notable for its unique talking drum solo, which Mick Fleetwood later embedded in the song during live performances. Unlike the usual drum solo, a sedentary flapping of drums sticks, these drum parts were turned into a whole-body experience by Fleetwood.

"Sugar Daddy," a workmanlike blues song by Christine McVie, follows. The album closes with Lindsey Buckingham's *pièce de résistance*, "So Afraid." The song had been conceived years earlier, and had been fully arranged in Buckingham's head, but at the time he felt that he did not have the equipment to frame the song in the way he wanted. It features a complex, three-part guitar harmony, and his old Fender Twin was not up to the task of carrying all those rare and precious notes. His vocal on the recorded song is raw and vulnerable, and the guitars crash and crescendo around him. Were it not for the vocal arrangement and subtle textures, the song would be a power ballad of Foreigner-like proportions—but Buckingham, as the band would find out over the years, rarely chose the road most traveled.

seedy management

In 1976 Mick Fleetwood and John McVie took out an ad in the U.S. music trade papers to declare that they had formally signed control of their life over to Seedy Management of Los Angeles. It was a wry joke on the band's part—in the picture, seated next to the rest of the band, dressed in a theatrically shady manner, were Fleetwood and McVie, holding pens.

It was a defiantly triumphant move on their part, explains writer John Grissim, who was then a freelance correspondent for *Rolling Stone*. A longtime follower of Fleetwood Mac's career, Grissim was one of few people given access to the inner realm of the studio control room while the band recorded *Rumours*.

In the summer of 1976, after the *Fleetwood Mac* album had, at last, gone to Number One in the U.S. charts, Mick Fleetwood told Grissim that people could no longer say that the band wouldn't make it without "heavy" management, such as the Eagles's übermanager, Irving Azoff. Obviously the band had made it, so that line was a little past its sell-by date. Now the sages of commerce were telling Fleetwood and McVie that they wouldn't be able to keep up with their success unless they sought outside counsel. McVie and Fleetwood refused to cave in to the fear.

"Most certainly, self-management was the right decision," affirms Grissim. "Mick had great leadership skills, and John was very good, too. They had a great deal of experience— nine years. They were business-like; they always delivered the product and had the right lawyers and accountants for the job. They didn't need what Van Morrison called 'pressure mongers,' which I think is a great term—they just needed to get on and make a really good album."

It was Fleetwood's opinion that a manager outside of the band's immediate family would not have been able to hold them together during the deep and chronic crises they experienced while recording their crucial follow-up album. Being both "Fleetwood" and "Mac," Mick Fleetwood and John McVie had a fair entitlement to this leadership role. Besides, Mick and John, the two band members who were not writers, and therefore, the two who did not enjoy the significant income that songwriting brings, needed to boost their own financial profiles.

Grissim recalls a humorous moment when a studio visitor made a bold move to unseat Seedy Management during the recording of *Rumours*: "I had a wonderful friend, a woman who was extremely bright. She had managed Dan Hicks, and she was a Lauren Bacall lookalike, extremely smart, a statuesque knockout. We were good friends, and she'd found out from me that I had entrée to the control room. She was about 40 years old, drove a white Mercedes, and wore minks; she knew rock 'n' roll, and I had a lot of respect for her. This was the only time I'd done this—I'd wrangled an invitation to get her into the studio.

"After a few minutes of conversation, in a session break, John McVie shows up, and I introduced them, explained who she was. And she said to John, 'Would you like a line?' And she brings out this Tiffany silver—it was like a bolt—and she unscrewed the top, and she produced a small mirror and lays out this really good-quality line. And she produces a four-inch-long, top-of-the-line Tiffany silver straw, and she hands it to John, who says, 'Thank you very much,' and he snorts the line. He's holding his nostril and she looks at him and says, 'Now that I've turned you on, I'd like to hit you up for management.' He laughed so hard he snorted the coke out of his nose. It was so funny—you know you're not going to get the job! It was a classic moment in rock 'n' roll. In retrospect, no, that's probably not how you hit up Fleetwood Mac for management."

Mick Fleetwood's dealings with Warner Brothers after the Clifford Davis calamity had given him some helpful practice for his negotiations with the record label in mid-1975. The entire band was thrilled with their new album; they heard something special there, something they felt the record buyers would hear, too, if only they knew about it. The label had been content in the past to allow Fleetwood Mac to do its thing without interference or help, to tour and find new guitarists, and to tour again, with the albums coming as surely as did the seasons. There hadn't been a great deal of marketing strategy, and the band decided that now would be a good time to spend the extra money on such a thing. Buckingham and Nicks were certainly ready for this experience, having seen their lovingly-crafted debut sink without trace in 1974. So Fleetwood and Shapiro arranged to meet with Warner Brothers to discuss this. They were fortunate to be dealing with one of the industry's best-respected executives, Morris Meyer Ostrofsky, known in the business as Mo Ostin.

Mickey Shapiro admires Mo Ostin to this day: "A nice guy? He was beyond that—a combination of intelligence and kindness, of creativity and commercial sense; a marvelous human being. He's not related [to me]—he's not paying me to say this [laughs]. I hope I could say I made that contribution and treated people as nicely if I was ever rich and powerful, which I probably won't be. He is an extraordinary guy."

Ostin came to the Warner Brothers empire when it bought Reprise, the company he worked for, from its owner, Frank Sinatra. In turn, Sinatra had found the former accountant at the jazz-oriented Verve label. To complement the skills of Ostin, Warner Brothers brought on board a sharp-witted Boston DJ named Joe Smith as head of promotion. The two men were well trained in commerce, but both were also appreciative of music and the creative process, which lent them considerable artistic credibility.

The new executives began signing rock acts, including the Kinks, Jimi Hendrix, the Grateful Dead, and Van Morrison. Ostin, especially, was willing to give artists free rein, reasoning that profits would follow naturally if the product was not vandalized by the ungroovy influence of the corporate bottom line. Both men also showed flexibility, which was quite remarkable for those still-staid times. Smith recalls buying Van Morrison's contract from a scary Mafia-like entity in the dead of night, and jumping two stories to his getaway car as soon as he took possession of the document. Nine of out ten bands would agree that this showed a remarkably giving approach to negotiation, and an enviable commitment to the artist.

The Warner Brothers company added yet more labels when it came under the management of a relative newcomer to the entertainment industry. Steve Ross had previously made his mark in the business of funeral parlors and parking lots. Under Ross, Atlantic, Elektra, and Asylum were added to the Warner Brothers empire, but, although they shared the company's distribution network, the individual labels were otherwise in competition with each other.

Ostin was not a showboating kind of media executive; quite the opposite. He got on with his work, rarely attended trade functions, gave interviews even more rarely, and his picture was seldom printed in the papers. There is a widely held perception that Warner Brothers, in particular Mo Ostin, was the most rock band-and-artist-friendly label of the 1970s. Al Kooper, who, in addition to being a musician, was an A & R man at Columbia Records in 1968 before founding the label Sounds of the South in 1972 to house the then-unheralded Lynyrd Skynyrd, partially agrees with this assertion: "[Mo Ostin is] a different personality perhaps, but Ahmet Ertegun and Clive Davis welcomed many Rock 'n' Roll Hall of Famers onto their labels as well. This includes the Stones, Aerosmith, [and] Led Zeppelin." Of course, Kooper drolly notes, Ostin did turn down Blood, Sweat & Tears, the blues-jazz-rock fusion band that he himself had founded in the late 1960s.

Los Angeles in the first half of the 1970s was dominated by the tastes of hippie conquistador David Geffen, whose fashionable Asylum label merged with Warner Brothers's Elektra label in 1973, thus forming a singer-songwriter folk-rock haven for a host of million selling SoCal artists. The Eagles' Asylum release "On the Border" sweet-talked its way to the top of the charts in early 1975 with its ornate post-country harmonies, and this paved the way for the sound of the new Fleetwood Mac later in the year. Jackson Browne and Linda Ronstadt released mellow, pretty music that sold in copious quantities. During the early 1970s, a new rock nobility had evolved from the ranks of dropouts who had moved into rustic L.A. canyon retreats at the end of the 1960s and early 1970s. Now they had moved to the beach and glammed out—although perhaps not in the way of David Bowie or Marc Bolan (that kind of glam was a much more British working-class drag revolution), but certainly in the way of extravagant lodgings and expensive drugs.

If one talks to people who worked out west in the entertainment industry of the 1970s, a common response is to recall the scene as a time of creativity, freedom, thrills, and fertile opportunity, rather like the 1960s with Stuff. "Well, compared to today, it was like Nero's Rome," remembers Al Kooper. "There were cartons of cocaine, willing women, and million-dollar press parties. The women are still there, but they're in their sixties now ... [Those were] druggy, orgy-filled times. I was the only rocker in L.A. who never did coke—I'm an insomniac and it was the wrong way for me to go."

Cocaine was broadly accepted in these circles as a social lubricant. Nicks has noted that it was customary to sit down with a journalist and share a gram, in the same way that one might have offered a guest a glass of wine. Accountants, lawyers, record executives, and artists snorted masses of the stuff, unaware of the awful damage it would later wreak. It powered the sound of Los Angeles in the mid-to-late 1970s, and Fleetwood Mac discovered its energizing, mood-masking properties while working on their White Album.

But unlike the story of Rhiannon's birds, after the blackout came raw reality. And the best cure for reality? More cocaine. Fleetwood Mac was not alone in spending untold thousands of dollars on the stuff, which they famously kept close at hand in a luxurious velvet pouch. A famous *Rumours* story concerns this same bag. As a joke, engineer Ken Caillat once replaced the bag with a similar one that was full of talcum powder. Caillat then "accidentally" spilled the powder all over the floor. As he pretended to salvage the powder (while making matters worse), the band freaked. They kept on freaking until producer Richard Dashut finally explained the prank, and order was restored.

Some of Fleetwood Mac's peers were accused of making sterile and bloodless albums under the effects of this cerebral overstimulation. Fleetwood Mac, who frequently worked in a state of deep trauma during their first two albums with Buckingham Nicks, found no amount of the old Peruvian marching powder could mute the heartache—although they certainly gave it the old college try.

When Fleetwood announced to the Warner Brothers team that the band would go out on the road before *Fleetwood Mac* was released, the label was not thrilled. Spending money before there was a major product to sell went against commercial policy. But Fleetwood and the others were so sure that the album was worth the extra effort that they went out anyway. Besides, this was Fleetwood Mac. They were a live band. Trying to keep them off the road would be like trying to keep a wave on the shore. It was the right move; Mickey Shapiro remembers the tour as "the birth of the big time" for the band. Fleetwood Mac found a brand new audience and blew them away. The record label, of course, had no idea that this would be the case. As far as it was concerned, Fleetwood Mac was just a reliable, faintly grubby blues band that had changed guitarists as often as other bands did hairstyles.

A little put out by Warner Brothers's muted response to their hard-won masterpiece, Fleetwood and Shapiro met with several other record companies, with a view to moving on after the band's contract with Warner Brothers expired. Fleetwood was determined to keep the band together; he always had one eye on the future. Many in his position would have wondered if there would *be* a future. Fleetwood Mac had taken a risk in bringing onboard two people who had previously functioned as a separate unit. The assimilation might have proved difficult, and, as far as Fleetwood knew, if one left, the other would too, causing twice as much disruption. In addition, the band was known for losing members on the road. And then there was the Clifford Davis fiasco. In 1976 Mick told *Rolling Stone* editor Ben Fong-Torres that the genuine Fleetwood Mac tour that followed the "Fauxwood Mac" debacle showed that significant damage had been done; concert halls which should have been full were not. Now the band was about to tour without a highly promoted product. Fleetwood took an unusual but most diplomatic step to mend the band's frayed reputation with concert promoters. Fleetwood and Courage agreed to give them money back whenever the box office takings put the promoter at a disadvantage. It was a good-faith gesture that they hoped would be returned the next time they went on the road. Seedy Management was confident in this gamble.

"Several British bands went out of their way to make it right for the promoters, and it was to their benefit later," remembers Michael Freeman, who was by now working as a tour manager in the United States. "Take Foghat, for instance—they always put on a great show and had great relationships with promoters—even if sometimes it seemed like they were always coming through town! You are in a business relationship with these people, and you hope it's going to be a long one."

Seedy Management learned to be creative with titles. They were convinced that the record company would not finance an outside promotions person, and they were undoubtedly correct; Mo Ostin was known to be opposed to the notion of independent promotion. Comments Michael Freeman, "I think Mo Ostin saw where it could lead, and that it was a dangerous road, a two-edged sword."

However, for the individual bands, in the short term it was an increasingly necessary marketing tool. Fleetwood Mac hired a promoter named Paul Ahearn and gave him the title of tour coordinator. This was true, in a way; it was his job to generate airplay for the band's next single in the markets in which they would be playing. The intent was to sustain their songs' radio airplay, and to make sure that when a single came out, the local stores had it in stock and the local media knew that the band was coming to town. It was Ahearn's suggestion to use Deke Richards to put together a car-radio, AM-friendly mix of "Over My Head," and it was a good one. Richards's new mix of the song was a key component in the band's breakthrough into pop radio. Meanwhile, back at Warner Brothers HQ, the company was still skeptical about the idea of the pub-stained blues band actually breaking out of its college FM niche. Even when the band's records began to sell beyond the label's projections, Warner Brothers refused to pay for such fripperies as promotional Fleetwood Mac balloons.

Mickey Shapiro remembers how the band had to push the record company into recognizing Fleetwood Mac's potential: "I think it was Mick who thought, 'This record's going to be a little different.' When we turned the record in, I talked to Bob Regehr and Mo Ostin, and said, 'How about giving us a full-page ad in *Billboard?*' 'Well, OK,' they said. And they put Lindsey's name under Stevie's picture and Stevie's name under Lindsey's, to show you how attentive they were. So the next week they ran the same ad with an arrow, showing 'Oops, we made a mistake,' which was characteristically Warner Brothers in those days—they were willing to laugh at themselves to make a point. That was Bob Regehr; he was brilliant. Around that time, Mick realized, 'Oh my God, they can't even get our names straight!' That's when they said, 'We've got to get our own record promotion guy'; then Ahearn came aboard."

The creative services division at Warner Brothers was run by Stan Cornyn, a man who was, and is, highly respected in the industry. In his book *Exploding,* Cornyn appears to overlook any efforts by the band to boost their profile, suggesting instead that Fleetwood Mac's "Over My Head" became a radio hit after a staff member named Linda York dissuaded Mick Fleetwood from buying a billboard advertisement in Los Angeles, and advised him to put the money into secondary radio ads instead. Shapiro holds Cornyn in high regard, but he disagrees with this analysis. Shapiro attributes the band's success to the impression they made during that first tour together: "They played their first gig together, and they were phenomenal. Stevie did her little dancing witch number, and from that moment on, young girls started dressing up like her. The radio may have had something to do with it, but the live performance—we didn't have boys and girls in bands together in those days. Here we had two pretty blonde girls and this odd-looking tall guy playing the drums [laughs], and then the other guys ... it was a very odd-looking group—not that it wasn't aesthetic, just that it hadn't been seen before.

"I did Steely Dan, and the Kinks before that, and God knows how many other groups. I went to that performance, and I remember coming home saying, 'I've seen a lot of wonderful groups play, but this is something different.' Generally when rock groups played, they appealed to the blatant sexuality the girls felt with some of the guitarists, that whole thing, and the boys kind of liked the aggressiveness of heavy metal music. [Fleetwood Mac] was a different thing. Girls weren't showing up because they were excited about having a sexual fantasy about the boys in the band; they wanted to be like Stevie Nicks. It was like, 'Whoa! What is this, this is not usual!' It wasn't like all the boys wanted to be Jimmy Page. They just thought it was cool."

The radio helped, but it would not have had the same effect without the band's accomplishments on stage. Fleetwood Mac was lucky to be reborn at a time when a few thousand dollars in radio promotion did make a difference. Three decades after the release of *Fleetwood Mac*, the landscape of rock radio in the United States has changed. Most of the popular radio stations are owned by a handful of powerful corporations, and independent radio stations are hard to find. One often hears the ironic observation that Top 40 radio actually has fewer than 40 songs on its playlist.

Michael Freeman remembers working with local radio stations in the mid 1970s, doing advance publicity for live shows: "The top pop radio stations could seem indifferent; you had to pull off some kind of dog-and-pony show for them. Then you had others that were born from independent radio, that weren't networked. They were music fans, and they listened to you; you actually talked to the program director or the DJ. You had a chance of getting on smaller stations, and there were many more of them. Grass roots are powerful forces if you work them properly."

In Fleetwood Mac's favor was the fact that three of its members were old hands at going on the road with a new lineup, and they were used to working out their problems in front of an audience. A band's creative growth is often accelerated by the process of public performance, and the band's egos allowed them to trip up a little in public. The stage was a space where the band blossomed. Even Mick upped his profile. He began taking the center of the stage to play his "talking drum" during "World Turning." The six-foot, six-inch minstrel was finally getting his rightful share of the limelight, banging out the blues and swinging his signature wooden balls, a bawdy talisman made from two wooden spheres borrowed from a pub lavatory chain.

The addition of another female to the band gave both Stevie Nicks and Christine McVie a place of refuge on the road. Christine and John had sealed their separation by occupying separate rooms on tour, and tension festered. The two women were vastly different in temperament and stage presence. McVie had been on the road long enough to earn the title of blues veteran. She was dry-humored and always ready to speak her mind if necessary. Although Nicks was theatrical and emotive onstage, offstage she could be a shy tea drinker—often huddled in a shawl, sketching or crocheting, conserving her energy for the draining two hours of performance—but she was always game for a laugh.

Both women shared a kindly, nurturing quality, as well as a willingness to accept the physical and emotional hardships of being on the road without a huge budget. They also shared the reality of being on the road with a partner with whom there was disharmony. (Although Lindsey and John might have been expected to commiserate with each other about their relationship problems, John tended to confide instead in his old friend, Mick Fleetwood.)

Nicks was touched by the way Christine graciously opened up the stage for her, a newcomer five years her junior, never showing what Christine later admitted were some instinctive territorial misgivings. Christine recognized Nicks's pure energy and saw how much it invigorated the band. Concert footage from this time shows McVie static, intent on tending her keyboards, stage right. Then there's Nicks, whipping around like a Gothic tumbleweed, and the two balance each other perfectly. This, they knew, was the truest thing of all, and it negated any feelings of rivalry between the two. If anything, it seemed that the one having the difficulty with Nicks's blooming persona was her long-term partner, Buckingham.

Nicks was also criticized by the occasional jaded journalist. In the beginning, Stevie Nicks got a few rough reviews that left her, not surprisingly, disheartened. In a 1977 *Rolling Stone* interview with Cameron Crowe, the journalist reported that Nicks was able to recite large sections of a bad review from that same paper, in which she was described as callow. However, in true Nicks tradition, she didn't quit. The band supported her by pointing out that the people who had actually paid to see the shows really, really liked her. This initial critical focus on Nicks was not surprising; she was putting a lot out there. It was a rather bold approach for a newcomer, but that was the only way she knew how to be. She soon disproved the critics' reservations.

The person responsible for helping Nicks realize her stage persona was celebrated L.A. designer Margi Kent, who met Nicks through another of her clients, George Harrison— Mick Fleetwood's brother-in-law. Says Kent, "Our first meeting we had about clothes was at her apartment, the duplex on Olympic in L.A. The first time I met her was at a rehearsal studio before their big tour, when they were first joining Fleetwood Mac. Stevie had a lot of input in as much as what she wanted to project, her affinity with soft, silky, chiffony things—things that had an iridescent, mystical quality. It was not what you would usually see in rock 'n' roll at all; it was a completely individual thing."

Nicks's gypsy-witch persona was instantly mimicable (and, of course, foxy enough to warrant mimicking), and the band gained in her a kinetic, dynamic visual that had been previously absent. "Rhiannon" became the band's signature set piece as Nicks, seemingly possessed by the spirit of the

Celtic wraith, spun and twisted across the stage, raven chiffon and silk whirling around her, as she danced as if under some terrible ancient obligation. Of course, Kent had designed these garments to allow movement, to do Nicks's bidding: "When you're doing any kind of costume, you have to take into consideration movement; it's not normal day-to-day wear. It's something that has to project a very small speck on the stage, to bring it forward. We wanted something that would create graphic shapes, that would be soft and fluid; that could change, so that when she wraps herself straight, it hangs lean, and when she spreads her arms, she can become very large and flowy. She was unbelievable on stage; no one did anything like that. She was completely spontaneous."

Nicks's top hat and mad Goth skirts were a bewitching convergence of history and myth and evoke the nineteenth-century windswept romanticism of the Brontës, the misty legends of the Middle Ages, Wiccan rituals, and fairy tales—all with an intriguing accent of Sunset Boulevard glam. Nicks was an independent female spirit who seemed not of this world, yet very much in it with her platform boots and frosted hair. Thousands of young women, newly awakened from the spell of patriarchy, saw in Nicks a way to live without sacrificing their "chickness" or "rockness"—to simultaneously express vulnerability and celebrate an earthy archetype.

And thus the band began to grow greater than the sum of its parts, and there a rebalancing of roles. Lindsey Buckingham had become part of a larger team, not just the leader of a twosome, and Stevie Nicks became a voice in her own right. Back in the British camp, the McVies were learning to live apart, and Mick played big brother to the two of them. Although it was a difficult time for the still-married pair, neither chose to leave the band.

The mid 1970s was a peak time for spotting Brits in Los Angeles. Apart from being the center of the recording universe, it has sunshine—a novelty that never wears thin for those born under Britannia's slate skies. At that juncture, in the days after glam rock, mainstream British rock and pop stars looked to Los Angeles for their sound and style. When they began making money, they moved there for the tax breaks. "The Rainbow and Rodney Bingenheimer's were the official British rock consulates in L.A.," affirms Al Kooper. Elton John, Mick Jagger, Keith Moon, and king of Malibu, Rod Stewart, spent a lot of time on the beautiful scene, while trying to diffuse the envy of those back home by complaining about "missing bangers and mash." In fact, the fierce passion of punk rock in the United Kindgom may have been born as much out of a desire to celebrate musicians who saw the beauty in their drab hometowns as it was from an urge to destroy the excess and indulgence that saturated rock culture.

The McVies and Fleetwood didn't fit in with the other rock-music expats in Los Angeles. They had come to the States as refugees—shopworn gentry who had been forced out of England by lack of money and the inability to find legal work, not because of a surfeit of highly taxable royalties. And they'd come with the intent of making the United States their home, where their hearts would be. Even Christine McVie, who so hated to leave her loved ones in England, was willing to give it a fair try. The wedding of these Brits and Los Angeles was a marriage of necessity, not of comfort. They were an American band, arriving in much the same way as that country's founding fathers had done, looking for the freedom to be themselves. It was not a little fitting that they were recognized as bona fide rock stars in the same year that America celebrated the bicentennial anniversary of the Declaration of Independence.

Lindsey's roommate, Richard Dashut, came back into the band picture around this time. A man with a reputation for being good-natured and accommodating, he was popular with all the band members. Dashut had been disappointed not to have been involved in the making of *Fleetwood Mac*, and when he was offered the job of mixing the band live, he accepted. This had been one of John Courage's tasks, and before Courage, it had been the job of the equally legendary roadie and sound installation king, Dinky Dawson. Courage was certainly professional enough to step aside, but not without giving Dashut a good initiation, which apparently involved a lot of sleep deprivation.

"Over My Head" charted in November 1975 and headed into the Top Ten. The Christmas of 1975 looked a whole lot different than the previous year's holiday. The band who supposedly could only sell 300,000 copies and no more, had sold a million and a half, giving them enough leverage to re-negotiate their contract with Warner Brothers (who were presumably now willing to buy the band all the promotional balloons that their hearts could desire). In addition, Buckingham and Nicks were officially inducted into the musical partnership.

Buoyed by the success of the album, Reprise went on to release "Rhiannon" in early 1976, which also hit the Top Twenty (much to Nicks's relief), and a third single, the bouncing "Say You Love Me," which also charted. By July, a year after its release, *Fleetwood Mac* had reached the number one slot in the U.S. charts. Over in the United Kingdom, the album made less of a connection with the public, and the album peaked at Number 23 in November 1976. Still, the little blues band that could was now responsible for Warner Brothers' best-selling album ever, and Fleetwood Mac was now officially part of the platinum record nobility that was dominated by the Eagles, Peter Frampton, and Boz Scaggs.

But there was no time for lounging around. The band was clearly hitting its creative stride, and its members were keen to start another album. Obviously, Warner Brothers was right behind this notion. Fleetwood began to look for a new studio to record in. In a question-and-answer session with the Internet site *The Penguin*, Keith Olsen recalled that a dispute over royalties, the eternal thorn in rock's side, had caused a cooling of his relationship with the band, although he stayed in touch with Stevie Nicks.

Mick Fleetwood saw his decision to seek out a new recording venue as a practical necessity. The tensions between the various band members needed to be counterbalanced. To do this, Fleetwood decided to take everyone out of their comfort zones—if that's what the previous months of arguments and painful silences could be called—by putting them in a new environment. In February 1976 the band and crew repaired to a studio called the Record Plant, sister studio to the Record Plants in New York and Los Angeles, in the San Francisco Bay-area town of Sausalito.

Mick Fleetwood's choice of Sausalito as an escape from the distractions of Los Angeles was an informed one—it wasn't as if he'd booked them into an Iowa farm town. Bob Edwards, now an Emmy-winning sound designer at George Lucas's Skywalker Sound, was, in the early 1970s, an engineer at the Sausalito Record Plant. He has very happy memories of time spent there: "Sausalito was a magical place back then, as evidenced by the rainbow painted over the entrance to the Waldo Tunnel, which welcomes you to Sausalito and Marin County. The fog, the redwood trees, the hills crawling with rock stars, Mount Tamalpais, Muir Beach and Stinson Beach, the Sausalito houseboat community, the bookstores and water-front bars and restaurants, all with lingering traces of beatniks and other miscellaneous hipsters—it was a very special time and place. Definitely laid-back, casual, funky, affordable, with an undercurrent of 'something special's going on here.'" The scene in Sausalito was about to get even more special.

sausalito dreaming

Drive north along Highway 101 across San Francisco's Golden
Gate Bridge to Richardson Bay in exclusive Marin County and
you will find the small but (now) very expensive coastal town
of Sausalito. The secluded coves along the shoreline once
made it an ideal place for ships to take onboard both legal and,
during prohibition, illegal provisions. Artists later colonized
the area, taken by its quaint architecture and fulsome natural
beauty. By the early 1970s Sausalito had become a favorite
hangout for the Bay Area's rock elite. Bob Edwards remembers
the unique music scene of that time: "[The music scene was]
mostly small clubs and bars—Sweetwater in Mill Valley, the
Lion's Share in San Anselmo, for example—and it was more
musicians playing for their friends and peers than huge, hero-
worship concerts. Van Morrison, Hot Tuna, scaled-down
versions of Jefferson Starship and the Grateful Dead come
to mind. There was a real sense of community, a very unique
and laid-back in-crowd."

San Francisco was very different from Sausalito. "Driving
across the Golden Gate Bridge definitely required an
attitudinal adjustment. At least that was my perception,"
recalls Edwards. "Larger clubs, more nightlife, more hustle
and bustle. I preferred slower-paced, greener Marin, but if
you had to live near a big city, San Francisco was definitely
the best choice on Earth at the time."

John Grissim, a San Francisco-based writer who reported
on the making of *Rumours* for *Rolling Stone* and *Crawdaddy*

magazines, remembers the Trident, one of the town's focal points. It was a waterfront restaurant that had been started by the manager and one of the partners of superstar 1960s folkies the Kingston Trio: "Oh my God, you'd go in there and it was fresh vegetarian food, this beautiful dock, the women all wore beautiful gossamer dresses with no bras, the waitresses were to die for! And hip royalty like David Crosby and Stephen Stills and Neil Young—it was when hip was in full flower—but money hip."

The Record Plant in Sausalito was the third studio opened by the happening team of businessman Chris Stone and the celebrated wild man of 1970s audio engineering, Gary Kellgren. "Gary was a very unique individual," remembers Bob Edwards. "He created exceptionally comfortable, experimental, trouble-free, 'anything-goes' environments." He drove (or was driven around in) a banana-yellow Rolls Royce that occasionally made its way up Interstate 5 to Sausalito. It was hard to miss, not only because of its color, but also because its personalized license plates sarcastically read "GREED."

The Sausalito Record Plant opened in 1972 to a star-spangled reception that was attended by the likes of John Lennon and Yoko Ono. Grissim has vivid memories of the studio's unique function and memorable decor, which echoed the design of its sister studio, the Record Plant in L.A.: "The invitations to open that studio were on carved pieces of redwood in the shape of a crescent moon, with everything airbrushed."

David Mitchell, the principal contractor and carpenter responsible for the Trident's design, also worked on the

Record Plant's design. "They created this by-the-water-front recording facility that was literally between yacht marinas, right off 101," continues Grissim, "very close to the water-front, very private—no windows. It wasn't a factory look either; it was shaded, with trees, a wood exterior with a cedar roof, very discreet. There were two big studios, top dollar, beautifully done, in the fashion of elegant hip, and of course it had every imaginable amenity including a hot tub, and some kind of room that was designed for people to sit around on these curved, long, puffy benches. It was so beautifully done. Everything was—puffy, and not Naugahyde but corduroy, and complementary to what was considered ultra, wonderful, California hip."

It was a place for bands to escape the relentless business world of Los Angeles without sacrificing their sophisticated tastes. "The Record Plant was L.A. technology and money, and Northern California cool hip," says Grissim. "What they also had, which was very cool, was a five-bedroom home nestled in Mill Valley, so musicians such as Crosby, Stills, Nash & Young, Sly Stone, and Stevie Wonder could stay at the Record Plant's private, hillside, ranch-style hacienda if they wanted to. They didn't get any bodyguards or anything, but people *loved* it! The Record Plant during the 1970s was a huge hit maker; people came from everywhere. There were two really good studios. They understood how to protect stars, how to protect celebrity."

Nina Bombardier has been the studio manager at Fantasy Studios in Berkeley, California for more than 20 years. However, back in 1976, then known as Nina Urban, she was the studio manager at the Record Plant in Sausalito and the designated project manager for *Rumours*. "Really, it was one of those boutique studios," she explains. "By having two locations [in L.A. and Sausalito], the owners had more flexibility in accommodating the bands, and could shuffle the overdubs or mixing between the two facilities."

Bob Edwards well remembers this period, which, looking back, seemed so carefree and spontaneous. "Record Plant staff engineers and assistant engineers regularly shuttled back and forth between the Los Angeles and Sausalito facilities. As a matter of fact, there was a period of time when I was engineering daytime sessions in Sausalito and nighttime sessions in L.A. [This was] thanks to the SFO helicopter, which took less than 20 minutes to get from the Sausalito helipad to the San Francisco airport, and PSA Airlines which allowed you to literally run full speed onto the plane and purchase your ticket *after* takeoff. Try that today!"

The facilities at the Record Plant were so carefully chosen that the members of Fleetwood Mac didn't need to leave the premises, except to sleep—although, according to Mick Fleetwood, sleep at this time was very often in short supply. Bombardier recalls the facilities on offer at the Record Plant, "We had a vending machine that sold Coors beer at 25 cents … a recreation room, a kitchen, a Jacuzzi, a shower; it was very comfortable. There was even a liquor store, the Bottle Shop, that delivered. Sometimes we would hire a cook to come in and cater—though Fleetwood Mac really didn't use one—and there was a lovely little patio out back. Eddie Money used to wash his car there, a dark brown Mercedes. Well, people needed to take a break from the studio. There weren't many windows, it was kind of dark."

This dream studio was a long way from the facilities that Peter Green's Fleetwood Mac had first encountered. "You could mistake a typical recording studio built in the 1950s and 1960s for a high school cafeteria or hospital," laughs Bob Edwards. "Very sterile and uninspiring—engineers isolated behind glass holes in the wall, lots of wires, switches, meters, and technicians with horn-rimmed glasses and pocket protectors. Gary and Chris changed all that with the design and staffing of the L.A. and Sausalito studios. They broke down the psychological barrier between the control room and the studio by making the window very wide, almost floor-to-ceiling height, and curved so as to 'bulge' out into the studio space. There were no clocks in sight and very few windows, the idea being to create an isolated and carefree creative environment. This was great for the musicians, but sometimes grueling for the staff, who occasionally found themselves staying up for days on end when inspiration struck."

The Record Plant in Sausalito—now known as simply the Plant—had almost as many incarnations as Fleetwood Mac, including one famous period in the 1980s, after it had passed through a couple of new owners (Stone sold the studio after Kellgren's untimely death in the late 1970s). "The federal government operated the studios for a while," confirms Bob Edwards, "when the next owner was arrested and imprisoned on drug-related charges. They did a shockingly good job, and the studio was nicknamed 'Club Fed' for a time."

John Grissim recalls his first encounter with Stevie Nicks during the *Rumours* sessions. "There was a nice little kitchen, a little galley—that's where I first met Stevie and Lindsey ...

When I first met Stevie Nicks, I didn't know her. I said something like, 'Really nice to meet you, Sheila,' and she said, 'It's *Stevie*,' in this throaty voice—I will never forget that," he laughs. "Because she came from a privileged background, she had that aura of confidence and entitlement, and that's not meant as a criticism."

The male members of the band stayed at the studio's two houses, one five-bedroom and one six-bedroom, overlooking Mill Valley. Nina Bombardier's duties also included overseeing operations at these two houses. "I even made the curtains on my own sewing machine. It wasn't like a 16-room Hollywood mansion, but they were nice, contemporary homes—lots of wood paneling, with one wall all glass, with a beautiful view over the valley—but not a lot of furniture, quite basic in that way." Meanwhile, Stevie and Christine took apartments in a condominium building by the Marina, rooms that Christine described to then-*Rolling Stone* reporter Cameron Crowe as strange "hospital" rooms. None of the puffy corduroy persuasions of the Record Plant's interiors for them!

Most of the recording of *Rumours* took place in Studio B, although Bombardier also remembers they worked in Studio A from time to time. The facility also housed other rooms, including the celebrated Pit, its amphitheatre-like layout described by Al Kooper as resembling something out of the film *Mad Max Beyond Thunderdome*, and Sly Stone's "bedroom," where Nicks spent a lot of time writing songs between takes.

"In the back of the Record Plant, we built a room for Sly Stone and called it 'the Pit,'" says Nina Bombardier. "It was actually dug into the ground—a smaller, looser-type setup, not a traditional studio with a control room; the console was right in the same room with the musicians, down in the Pit. They did mostly live stuff in there. Sly didn't own it; he was a long-term customer—he was under contract to Columbia Records but he didn't want to work under their watchful eye in their studios. The Record Plant owners were willing to accommodate all this. If somebody came to me now and said, 'I want to book your room for two years, but we want to put in a different console, move the furniture,' I'd say, 'Sure, let's see what we can come up with together to make you happy.'

"Studios A and B were about the same size. They looked a little different—almost like mirror images of each other, separated by a hallway. The control rooms were the same size. Studio B still looks pretty much the same today—wood floors in there, tie-dyed and paisley print baffles hanging from the ceiling, a mirror with a wood frame in the shape of a person playing the piano—very colorful and multishaped room. A was the same size, but the ceiling was a floating sky with clouds, a different vibe. I remember them being in both rooms."

It was into this world of Sly Stone's interior-decorating whims and Fleetwood Mac's newly single band members that John Grissim plunged in March 1976. He had just returned from a trip around the world, in part to recover from a heart broken by "Of all people, Van Morrison's estranged wife." At this time the band was big, but were not yet the gilded royalty they would become. "Fleetwood Mac had made an impact, but they had somehow slipped through the cracks. I had weird taste; 'Station Man' was one of my favorites. I was into them because I was into FM underground."

Grissim found that there was an art to hanging out with a band, especially a band that was in such vulnerable shape.

"I tried to cultivate the qualities of a really good groupie," chuckles John Grissim, "and a really good groupie doesn't tell you they're a groupie, they just make you feel comfortable, make you feel fuzzy. I treated them with respect and valued their privacy, and I sense that's why *Rolling Stone* hired me as a freelancer; I was kind of a guy they could hire when they didn't have the budget to hire one of their in-house writers to try to track down some rock star who kept hanging up on them, someone leery of the press. They'd say, 'Send Grissim; he'll find a way to meet them in a bar and we won't have to pay for it.' The band was just trying to work stuff out; they really hadn't had a whole lot of exposure, and I was really the only guy knocking on the door. *Rolling Stone* has some cachet, and they let me in. I immediately liked Mick Fleetwood; he was a real pro."

Grissim still had a lot of material left over. "I had recorded everything and taken copious notes," says Grissim of his extended visit to the Record Plant. "I immediately turned around and contacted *Crawdaddy*, because at that time they were the only magazine that offered a market for this kind of long thing—it was a cover story. *Crawdaddy* was very good, intellectually sound and thoughtful, focused on music—I had great respect for them—and they said, 'John, go for it, go *New Yorker* length.'"

Details from this article went on to form the basis of many of Mick Fleetwood's reminiscences of this time for his auto-biography, and it was in it that Grissim made the observation, "One might have questioned [Fleetwood Mac's] wisdom in allowing an observer access to the studio during those hectic weeks." However, Grissim now concludes, "They obviously felt strong enough as a band to have a journalist from a major rock paper there.... It became clear that there might have been a little bit of bedroom nonsense happening at the house—but they also knew they had an opportunity to record a really good album. They were really excited to be there, and knew they had something special with Lindsey and Stevie, and even though things were a bit wobbly between them, they showed up every day and got it done."

The band was ready to try a more open-ended approach to recording after the more disciplined experience at Sound City. Because of interpersonal strife, the band was in an emotionally fragile state and needed to define their creative space as they went along. In addition, Buckingham, after working as part of a team during the recording of *Fleetwood Mac*, was anxious to stretch himself, and to have a greater influence over the recording process. Although they did appoint an external producer, Richard Dashut, he was not seen as an outsider by the band. He was a close friend of Buckingham and got along well with all of the band members. He was an artistic facilitator: he complemented their vision, rather than asserting his own.

In all of this, the band was fortunate enough to have the support of the record company, a luxury denied to other bands who had to be content with record company staff producers stopping by. Some of these staff producers knew what they were doing, recalls Bob Edwards. Others, however, would be more interested in calling prospective dates while sitting at the console as the music played. Edwards remembers, "One guy would occasionally ask us to clip a couple of sunlamps to the ceiling of the control room so he could sit next to the engineer with shades on and get a tan while he 'worked.' I'm not kidding!"

Fleetwood's autobiography notes that the original chief engineer on *Rumours* was let go because he was "too into astrology." Bombardier does not recall the Sausalito Plant being involved at this stage, and assumes it was someone from Los Angeles. Cris Morris, who served as engineer on the entire project and who got a production credit on the album, says, "Deke Richards, who mixed 'Over My Head,' which was a hit, wanted to do this next album, naturally. They decided to go with Ken Caillat, who was more of a novice, because Deke kind of wanted to take over, and I don't think they wanted that. They wanted to do it themselves, pretty much."

The band was ready for a little more freedom after its more regimented, budget-driven experience at Sound City. "Oh, that was a whole lot of stuff," laughs Morris, who had met Fleetwood and the McVies when they were recording at Angel City in Los Angeles. Morris came to *Rumours* straight from working on Stevie Wonder's *Songs in the Key of Life*. He had begun work in the industry at Roulette Records in New York and then moved to Los Angeles, where he worked at the Record Plant. He heard of the new business up north: "I knew they were building a studio. I started out cleaning toilets, I was a carpenter—we built the studio from the ground up; I hammered nails into the walls. It was all custom work."

Richard Dashut had originally come along to Sausalito as Buckingham's companion. He claims he never intended to be a producer. This would be his first time as a solo producer, and what a way to begin. Mick took him out into the Record Plant parking lot, which served as a kind of forum for extra-studio discussions and disagreements, and told him he, Dashut, was now the producer. Dashut decided he needed some extra technical expertise, and he summoned a pal from the Wally Heider Recording studios in Los Angles, Ken Caillat.

Dashut is invariably described by those who have known him as modest, good-humored, and patient. Musician Jeff Murphy, whose band Shoes worked with Dashut shortly after *Tusk* was produced, recalls a man always ready to forgive others for their foolhardy behavior—even if it resulted in damage to Dashut or his property. He was also ready to do almost anything for a laugh. Murphy remembers Dashut falling face first into a plate of spaghetti. "He was a practical joker who really seemed to love being part of a team, rather than being a dictator," remembers Murphy. Keith Olsen, producer of *Fleetwood Mac*, remembers his former second engineer as "a really great guy, a nice guy."

Dashut's sunny nature and upbeat approach would have been invaluable in keeping together the five musicians and their frayed nerves and broken heartstrings. One can only imagine how tired his "smile muscles" must have been at the end of the sessions. He has stated that his strong points are the ability to communicate with people, to keep momentum, and provide creative perspective. He modestly saw his role on the *Rumours* project, and that of Caillat, as keeping things running and making sure the instruments were tuned. Lindsey Buckingham noted in a 1992 interview that Dashut would help him see the larger vision when he became swamped by minutiae.

Ken Caillat, a gifted studio engineer, first met up with Dashut when the latter booked himself into Wally Heider's studio to remix some live Fleetwood Mac tapes in 1975. They got along famously. Caillat is known for having an eye for technical details, as well as for fixing and inventing equipment. In later years the California resident developed a patented device called the Quake Awake, an earthquake detection system. The *Rumours* production team was rounded out by Cris Morris, the in-house engineer who had helped build the Record Plant in Sausalito.

In theory, with Fleetwood Mac's steady ascent toward that platinum star, 1976 should have been a good year for the band. But, as was noted by the philosopher Boethius, fortune is a complex beast, a series of wheels within wheels, each following its own path. While the band's commercial fortune was on an upward swing, the wheels of their personal lives were spinning mercilessly downward and taking everybody with them. The April 22, 1976 issue of *Rolling Stone* reported that Nicks and Buckingham were the second couple in Fleetwood Mac to be treading choppy waters, noting that Christine and John McVie had split up eight months earlier. To further complicate matters, Mick Fleetwood's 12-year marriage to Jenny Boyd was headed for the divorce courts.

Nicks admitted that she and Buckingham had been ready to break up even before they joined the band. They hung on, knowing that if they broke up in those first six months, the band would also fall apart. Fleetwood told writer James McNair in 2003 that it was Nicks who had pulled away emotionally, making life in the band difficult for Buckingham initially. He complained to Fleetwood that he had to "make Nicks's music," and was not able to have closure. Nicks has contended in other interviews that Buckingham had become increasingly critical of her flamboyant stage persona and of her appeal to the lusty men of America. When they finally split, she said, it was no less hard for her; she just tried to keep things on an even keel for the good of the group. In those early days in Sausalito, it was all they could do to box up the anguish and stuff it into the basement of their minds.

In his autobiography, Mick Fleetwood sums up the general tenor of the band's intrapersonal dealings, saying that they spoke to each other in "clipped, civil tones in airless rooms." The tension was an undercurrent they tried to keep under control while working in the studio. Outside the studio, tempers flared. Both Stevie Nicks and Christine McVie recall hiding in each other's rooms at the Marina condominium while their respective exes roamed the hallways, looking for them. Mick Fleetwood often found himself in the middle of disputes, such as the time he had to tell Stevie Nicks that her beloved song "Silver Springs" would not be included on the album. And who was there to help Fleetwood in his hour of need? Richard Dashut, of course. Dashut, interviewed for VH1's *Behind the Music*, affectionately recalls Mick Fleetwood collapsing into his arms when the going got too much.

In speaking with Cameron Crowe about the emotional agonies of the Sausalito sessions, Christine McVie used the word "trauma" to describe the spiritual abrasion of those all-night-and-all-the-next-day-too recording sessions. Christine and the band's lighting director, Curry Grant, were at that point romantically linked. Although she and John had officially split, it still was awkward for Grant to be in the studio when John McVie was around, perhaps more so, thought Christine, than it was awkward for her when John brought new girlfriends into the studio. He certainly tested this theory when he showed up one day in the company of Peter Green's former girlfriend, Sandra. For his part, Richard Dashut claimed that there was a time when he slept under the mixing console at the Record Plant because he felt it was the only safe place around.

Cris Morris remembers, "Mick was having his troubles with his wife. I thought he wrote a good book; he didn't get too raunchy with it. He could have gotten a lot more. He was a gentleman, I thought, about everything. He has great strength and good character, and that's his due. He managed the band—it took a lot of strength and he went though plenty of his own problems trying to keep his family together. He did devote 100 percent to the band; he and John never really stopped from the 1960s onward. They kept pushing on. Most people could never really get that far, with all the adversity, especially with the people, the family-type relationships."

John Grissim noted in *Crawdaddy* that the band was not ashamed of the romantic turmoil. Nicks has said that if she has something interesting to say, she doesn't mind sharing her personal life. Buckingham was also open about the emotional struggles, pointing out to Cameron Crowe that, just because they may be appointed rock stars, it didn't mean they didn't go through the same heartache and dysfunction as anyone else. Their close proximity gave the couple little headroom or neutral ground. As Nicks told John Grissim, ending their romantic relationship was the only option, since neither of them was able to be creative otherwise.

Nicks and Buckingham have both acknowledged that when creative and musical frustrations set in, the artistic friction made it hard for the relationship end of the partnership to function, and vice versa. Nicks mentioned being too vexed to console Buckingham after a day of his being unable to get a part right, and that he in turn might have been less inclined to work out a truly beneficial arrangement for one of her songs if they had had an argument. For this, she had to depend on his goodwill toward her, making the creative process something of a minefield to negotiate.

Buckingham's talent for arrangement has been described by band members as a sprinkling of enchanted fairy dust, where he takes an ordinary, downtrodden chord sequence, works his magic, and sends it, sparkling, to the ball. Buckingham feels he has a natural affinity for arranging Nicks's work, and no one will argue with him on this point. In turn, Nicks's ear for the meter of language matched Buckingham's grasp of the meter of music. The beautifully paced simplicity of her lyrical phrasing and the simple lines of her melodies gave Buckingham the space he needed to add detail and dynamics to the songs.

The two never wrote a song together—neither as Buckingham Nicks nor as Fleetwood Mac. As mentioned earlier, when Buckingham and Christine McVie worked together on "World Turning," Nicks described feeling somewhat hurt. Actually, "World Turning" was a rare collaboration for the band—its three songwriters usually worked alone, and each had an individual style: McVie was poppy and soulful, Nicks was mystic and folkyish with a little bit of Nashville, and Buckingham was as angry a young man as one could hope to find among the waterbeds and suntans of Los Angeles. The arrangements of all the band's songs were often adjusted by Buckingham, who also edited lyrics for length. However, each individual had a distinct personal narrative style—McVie, purveyor of heartful pop metaphors; Nicks, painter of poetic archetypes; and Buckingham, the acerbic venter—so the demands of any of them collaborating on a lyrical theme would be hard to reconcile.

In his *Crawdaddy* article, John Grissim wonderfully described the evolution of a parallel social world of studio visitors, who showed up around the band whilst pretending they were not in the least bit interested in the proceedings. The local hip crowd would hang out at the well-appointed studios, drawn by the presence of the increasingly happening band. He noted their studied nonchalance as they encountered real Fleetwood Mac band members in the hallways, pretending not to notice them: "[It was] a two-way procession, like some weird unbonded double helix." The band generally seemed to have no idea who all the people were, preoccupied as they were with their own swirling tides of angst. Other musicians also dropped by, some of whom were using the studio facilities. These included Chaka Khan, Rick James, Jackson Browne, and the band's old friend, Warren Zevon.

Mick Fleetwood has described the drug-ridden, angst-laden recording of *Rumours* as the craziest part of their lives—not a comparison to be taken lightly. Richard Dashut has admitted he thought he might go mad with the sleeplessness and the carrying on. And as for the house in Mill Valley, "Gawd 'elp you, what went on there!" laughed Mick in one interview, thereby painting a picture more vivid and intriguing than any list of debauched Bacchanalian detail.

But it was not always madness; certainly not during daytime hours. Nina Bombardier remembers days of relative calm and normalcy: "They had to walk by me every day. They came to me for help—we didn't hang out and get high. I wasn't the type, and most of that was kept inside the studio. In any of the studios then, it was mostly kept private. Sometimes they would get nothing done; other times were really productive.

"They frequented the restaurants, and the local pubs," says Bombardier. "It was a pretty cool place to hang out— beautiful views of the water. I don't think they did a whole lot more. When people were making records, they spent a good amount of their waking time in the studio. They didn't go to movies or to San Francisco—you were in the studio from noon to midnight, then you'd go home, do whatever you were gonna do, and come right back to the studio. When you're in a little town like Sausalito, you do get to know the people; there's dating, but it was just normal stuff."

Lindsey Buckingham has noted that the band didn't really have any of the album worked out prior to going into the studio. Nowadays, it seems quite extraordinary that a band would be allowed to block so much open-ended time in an expensive studio without demo tapes to prove they knew what they were doing. But Bombardier says it was typical of the times: "The attitude was, 'what do you need?' There was a recognition that music is a living, breathing thing that needs time to grow; five days was not always enough!"

Buckingham has always considered himself more of a stylist than a musician, preferring to go in to record with just fragments, which are then given form and dimension as the studio clock ticks. In an interview with *Performing Songwriter* magazine, he described how the concept of a song could change as one new part affected the way in which the other parts interacted, which is clearly why Buckingham has always had a preference for being at the wheel, making adjustments and changing direction on the fly. Without this flexibility, "The Chain" would never have risen from the ashes of one of Christine McVie's discarded songs.

According to Keith Olsen, such freedom was a double-edged sword where Buckingham was concerned: "Lindsey's true creativity, and his dedication to creativity, is a curse and a blessing because it's the sort of thing that could make him grow crazy if it doesn't feel 100 percent right. He'll never be happy. So many moments in that album were all about heart and creativity. About dedication to that creativity and to the potential that all of us have, 'let's just keep at it and we know that it'll be there.' Don't over analyze it and spend 23 days on a guitar part because it's there! Gee, there's a little mistake in it, I know, but that's heart and soul, that's real.

"That was one of the things that took me aback on the *Rumours* album—that every single thing was thought out. Now there's a huge market for thought-out music, [laughs]. But when there's great songs like the great songs they have on *Rumours*, you don't need to think out every single thing." Olsen laughingly warms to his theme: "I read an interview once where they said they spent 21 days on a guitar part. Well, he should be *shot* for doing 21 days on a guitar part, especially that little part they were talking about!"

A lesser problem for the band was the issue of the record label. Fleetwood has mentioned that he had to struggle to keep eager ears at Warner Brothers at bay. Bombardier recalls that the label always paid the studio without any trouble, but she says, "I know there was concern on Warners' part that the bills were mounting. They [the band] pretty much booked the studio on a 'lockout,' which means they have that particular room exclusively. They at least booked it by the week, if not the month. They worked long days. Back then, prices were around $135 an hour, more than what people are getting now in a way: it was a 24-track studio."

At that time, 24-track recording technology represented the height of sophistication, and the cost of hiring such a studio reflected this. The machine allowed 24 separate parts to be recorded as layers on any given tape segment. In modern times, with the advent of easily affordable digital recording, it is easy to forget that the facility for seemingly unlimited overdubbing was once only the privilege of the rock elite. At that time, it was not common practice to send tapes of works in progress to the record company. "In those days, people would actually fly up and check on the tracking and mixing," says Bombardier. "It wasn't like these days, where everything gets sent overnight—there was no Fed Ex!"

John Grissim comments, "Warner Brothers would always want to hear something, wouldn't they? But I'm sure that all Mick had to do was woof at them, and they'd go away." The band moved back to Los Angeles in mid-March, and found themselves in much closer proximity to the label. They closed the studio doors to all outsiders, in order to focus on the record that *they* wanted to make. Before they could continue, however, they had to deal with a technical problem of such magnitude that they first assumed they would have to start over from scratch.

lay me down
in the tall grass

In these days of digital audio, the accomplishments of the analogue heroes of old have dwindling meaning. The tape editors, who practiced for years running tape back and forward across tape heads to find a precise edit point, and the tape operators, whose fine-tuned aural and manual co-ordination created the precious skill of being able to drop a musician into the middle of a take to correct an error, relied on their ears and their hands. They did not have the luxury of viewing the sounds as digital waveforms that could be easily manipulated and mathematically calculated. Not only is analogue tape a difficult medium to manipulate with precision, but it is also a fragile canvas. It must be carefully stored, so that the sound images don't leak into the next layer of oxide, and it does not take kindly to being overworked.

Sometimes analogue is a deliberate and favored choice of some discerning factions within the audio arts—factions who find digital reproduction of sound to be, well, inhuman. Analogue sound is treasured for its warmth, its dither, its very mortality; in this world, the effect of the high end sloping off into the sunset is a thing of beauty. But it is a choice. Back in 1976, there was no choice, and analogue tape was a nightmare for Messrs Dashut, Caillat, and Morris.

After over 3,000 hours of recording, the 24-track Sausalito master tapes had lost a great deal of clarity and most of the high-end frequencies. Only the drum track and a couple of guitar tracks were considered viable. This was in the days before there was a method of automatically synchronizing two tape machines; in order to transfer the contents of an old tape to a new safety master, the machines had to be synchronized manually, a task of mind-warping dexterity and coordination. There was only one man to oversee the job: the future inventor of the Quake Awake. In the poky confines of ABC Dunhill Studios, in the blue-movie sector of Hollywood Boulevard, Ken Caillat and the studio's head of maintenance (a man whose name history has neglected to remember; Caillat believes he might have been named Jerry) accomplished this by listening through headphones to both tapes simultaneously and making manual adjustments when the sounds went out of phase—which meant the two tapes were no longer in synchrony. Caillat tried it himself for one song, he told *The Penguin*, and found it too grueling.

The Record Plant tape machine, famously nicknamed "Jaws" after the hugely successful movie of the previous year, took a lot of the blame; it was said that it chewed up the tape from time to time. Nina Bombardier is not so sure that the hardware was at fault at all. "Anybody who keeps playing the same tape over and over, month after month—the tape is eventually going to wear down," she laughed. "It becomes more vulnerable. Sure, they called it Jaws, but I don't believe it was the machine. I think it was the wear and tear on the tape from traveling over the heads so much."

Cris Morris remembers the transfer and the subsequent work very vividly: "It was kind of brutal; we had to wild synch a few things in. We had a roll of master tape. We'd worked on it so long that we'd started to lose the oxide off the back, and some of the fidelity was deteriorating. We had had new master dupes [made] early on in Sausalito. And at one point we decided we needed to transfer four or five songs off the album to the drum tracks from the original duplication, so we went from the tape we'd been using and synced over a lot of the tracks, onto the copy of the [original] drums. We had to take two multitrack machines, transfer it over, and hope that it locked in proper time."

Rumours was recorded at a number of studios; the band was at the Sausalito Record Plant from February 4 to April 9 of 1976 before breaking for a few tour dates that were made in order to keep momentum going with the *Fleetwood Mac* album. The band's usual work pattern had been disrupted. Recording an album had never taken this long, and now they had to deal with the need to promote the previous album while recording its follow-up, an album on which so many homes and year-end bonuses rested. The band ultimately had to cancel a string of fall dates in order to complete the new album.

After the Sausalito sessions, between rehearsing for their tour and actually touring, the band took off to Criteria Studios in Miami, but they were not there very long, according to Cris Morris: "I remember the hotel was all Spanish. It was a big Miami hotel, but no English was spoken at all. It was a little odd."

And so they returned to Los Angeles. The first recording sessions at Wally Heider Recording were logged on May 21, 1976 and the last session was held on August 19, 1976. Other sessions were recorded at Record Plant in Los Angeles,

Sound City in Van Nuys, and Davlen Recording in North Hollywood. The album was mixed at Sound City and at the L.A. Plant and it was mastered by Ken Perry.

Herbert Worthington III, the photographer for the *Rumours* album project, recalled in a feature for the magazine *Q* that Mick Fleetwood took away all the clocks in the studio so the band would not feel pressured by time passing. The studios did not have any windows to let in daylight, so this further shielded the band from time's cracking whip. Then there was Lindsey Buckingham and his refusal to accept anything less than perfection, especially of himself; it all made for a slow and detailed process. "Everything took a long time with that record!" says Cris Morris. "It might have been the most intense because we mixed singles from the previous albums as well. 'Say You Love Me' was mixed while we were recording. 'Over My Head' was mixed by Deke Richards, but the others were done by Richard, Ken, and myself."

Of all the tracks recorded, the band and the studio crew gave the most attention to the recording of the drum tracks. Cris Morris remembers spending 10 hours at the Sausalito Record Plant, working on a kick drum sound in Studio B, before they moved to Studio A, where they had built a special platform for the drums. This was the start of Fleetwood Mac's fondness for in-studio construction projects. Talking to Adam Budofsky in *Modern Drummer* magazine, Fleetwood remembers many failed experiments. One such "lunatic idea" was the attempt, in Sausalito, to tape three kick drums together. This was unsuccessful so instead they "just moved some mics."

"We spent days just doing the drum sounds," recalls Morris. "Every day was 15 or 16 hours, and we worked every day, with not really any time off. The band took a little time off, but not Lindsey. Stevie took a week off here and there, during the touring; Mick and Lindsey and Christine hung in there. The others might have taken some time off when it came to doing Lindsey's guitars in L.A."

Then there were the piano tuners. Says Nina Bombardier, "Christine needed a blind piano tuner. She wanted someone who totally tuned by ear. They did not *have* to be a blind person, but that was pretty much what we had to get in the end." Cris Morris has vivid memories of the tuner turnover: "We had so many piano tuners over that album, we wound up with a blind piano tuner from Berklee. I believe, over a two-month period, we had one for a week or so, then another. Usually they came in every day as part of the routine."

Christine was extremely dedicated to her art and rivaled Buckingham when it came to detail. "Christine spent every minute of every day there," remembers Morris. "I remember how much I've thought of her over the years as one of the hardest-working women I've been around, although there weren't a lot of women in those days in rock 'n' roll; they were there, but they were rarely that vital a part of a band. In northern California, it was just basically Grace Slick!"

Then of course there are the real reasons that everything took so long. It wasn't the clocks, or the perfectionism. It was the heartache, and the things they took to get through the agonizing days—bagfuls of cocaine and high-end alcohol. To recap, John and Christine McVie had just split up and during the recording of *Rumours*, Nicks and Buckingham finally broke up. Mick Fleetwood was not to be left out of the torture—he was in the process of again separating from his wife Jenny, the mother of his two children. Their fractured relationships caused excruciating tensions and undercurrents, and each band member struggled to hold himself or herself, as well as the band, together. But no one even thought of quitting—not that Mick would have let them had they tried.

That the band contained two couples in a state of painful flux could well have been a reason why the pain they felt worked for them rather than against them. It provided a kind of symmetry, a balance, and a strange sense of normalcy, especially because the fifth member, Fleetwood, was experiencing similar troubles. Had just one couple been at war, the proceedings may have spun off-center.

The situation also provided comradeship for most of those involved. John McVie and Mick Fleetwood gave each other support. Lindsey Buckingham might have seemed the obvious partner-in-consolation to McVie, but there was often creative tension between the two of them. Buckingham was more of a loner who lost himself in music rather than blind partying, and he already had a close friend in Richard Dashut.

Christine McVie and Stevie Nicks, meanwhile, provided support for each other. Those were the days before an extensive female entourage joined the band (Nicks later insisted on traveling with close female friends); Stevie and Christine just had each other. In an interview for *Backbeat*, conducted just after they had finished tracking the album, Christine commented that the wealthier they became, the better they were able to cope. The cash helped a lot— the ability to charter their own planes took off some of the pressure and gave them some space and a small sense of control.

Ken Caillat joked, in *The Penguin*, that he and Richard Dashut thought about wearing helmets to protect themselves. On the other hand, he doesn't feel the album would have been the same without the deep pain they experienced and the honest, almost innocent way in which they dealt with it. He contrasted the making of *Rumours* with the recording of *Mirage* in France, two albums later. By that time, decadence had set in; the band was overpampered and unhappy, and the team spirit of old had dissipated. While recording *Rumours*, however, despite the indulgences and excesses, they were not jaded, but simply sad, said Caillat.

In a 2003 interview with writer Gavin Martin, Fleetwood describes himself at that period as "the raver of ravers ... the next Keith Moon waiting to happen." That he survived, he later commented, was partly through the grace of the fates and because of the support given by his colleagues—and also because of the support he was able to offer others. Mick Fleetwood needed to be needed. Fleetwood, never far from his rather dark sense of humor, has commented a couple of times that he had considered giving his cocaine dealer a credit on the album. However, says Fleetwood, the dealer was executed on the street before the album came out.

Of course, there were also light-hearted moments. Cris Morris recalls the famous "thousand-dollar cookie session." One of Buckingham's girlfriends brought some marijuana-laced baked goods to the studio. They were so potent, and were so enjoyed by all, that the entire evening's session—at a cost of around one thousand dollars—was spent doing little in the way of recording. In fact, Stevie and John spent the night giggling in a corner over a girlie magazine.

Although Buckingham did decide, after his split with Nicks, that he was going to find companionship in other women, in 1992 he told writer Mat Snow that there was no "wife-swapping" during the recordings, as had been rumored. As for the drugs, although he was not a particular fan of them, he conceded that—given the band's schedule and the general mood—some chemical assistance was needed to function on a certain level—to get some cerebral energy, and to quiet the pain in their hearts and the whimpers of their ravaged body clocks.

"Everyone did pretty well in the studio," says Cris Morris. "Despite whatever feelings they had—which came out in the vocals—everybody was trying 100 percent because we knew it was going to be a big record."

and let me do my stuff

Rumours opens with "Second Hand News," which author Buckingham said had the working title of "Strummer" in honor of the choppy acoustic guitar accompaniment.

Mick Fleetwood's idea was to play the rhythm in a straightforward Celtic pattern. Buckingham, however, was very taken by a disco hit of the day—the Bee Gees' "Jive Talkin'"—and Fleetwood and McVie incorporated the seamless roll of its dance beat into the song. McVie added a rapid-fire syncopated bass. Rough versions of the song show how much effort Buckingham put into his vocal. He is slightly breathless as he pushes to fit, into one seamless take, the vigorous chorus and the syncopated scat singing in the chorus's tag. The final mixed version of the vocal has the breathlessness removed, but the energy intact.

Also in rough versions, one can hear Buckingham's splats of twisty distorted guitar, which blurt in, rather like the work of a painter who adds massive daubs of black paint to a picture and appears to be about to disfigure it, but who ends up shaping and blending the daubs into surprising shadows. Also featured on this track is a drum fill which was played on the back of a chair. The chorus features some of Fleetwood's best drumming—it's even, relentless, and glorious. The romping acoustic guitars, pounding piano, and rigorous vocals combine in the final mix as an exuberant and hyper-rhythmic whole. For those keeping count, this is a song by Buckingham about Nicks.

It is natural that Nicks would be allowed to respond, and she does so with the next song on the album, "Dreams." The emotional intent of the vocal is clear on unmixed versions of the track. Her line about women coming and going has a slightly dismissive edge to it, but the song as a whole Nicks saw as an ode to redemption and new beginnings, where the rain washed away the pain of the past.

Nicks wrote the song during a break from watching the others track their parts at the Record Plant. She'd discovered the notorious Sly Stone bedroom, and it was here, surrounded by her throat sprays and crochet work, in Sly's excessively appointed black-velvet boudoir, that she wrote her discreetly moody superhit. Nina Bombardier remembers the room that first bore witness to the song: "We built Sly a bedroom and a bathroom, and that was pretty wild. We built his bed—he wanted it to look like a mouth, so I had to do fur and make the entrance to the built-in bed in the corner like a pair of lips. The bedspread was made of black fur, and the lips were covered in red fur. Somebody else made that, but I had to buy fabric, get the carpenters, get them paid, and deal with the air conditioning company."

Nicks recorded the song, written in a mere five minutes, she says, onto a cassette so she wouldn't have to feel self-conscious actually singing it live in front of the rest of the band. In a 1992 magazine interview, John McVie recalls digging up Nicks's "Dreams" demo years later. He said that on it she can be heard saying, "This is how 'Dreams' goes," and proceeding to tap out the famous bass motif on the piano.

The song began as three separate parts, each composed of the same chords. "Quite boring at first," commented

Christine McVie during an interview for a *Rumours* retrospective. That was before Buckingham sprinkled his magic arrangement dust. John McVie's bass philosophy—keep the part as simple as possible, and leave a lot of space—is perfectly in play here, and his bass sounds sinister and brooding. Paying attention to the vocal, working around it—a habit acquired in the blues days of old—was the key to the success, and reputation, of this band's rhythm section.

Says Morris, "Most of the vocal was done with the drums; it was just her and Mick in the studio, which was very unusual in those days. We had to keep a lot of that vocal because it had the drum sound [embedded] in it. There was no guide guitar—we had a little keyboard she played while she was singing—it was just her voice and the drums. That was pretty interesting—that had never happened on any records I had worked on."

Caillat has commented in *The Penguin* that the band's songs were often recorded in a similar way: the writer would sit at his or her instrument, and the band would chime in. After capturing several takes, they might piece them together and then begin the overdub process—"the colors," according to Caillat, of guitars and backing vocals. In this song, a wonderful example of Buckingham's sense of shading can be heard in a subtle, sustained tone that sounds just before the chorus begins, and links the song beautifully without the link sounding intrusive.

After the addition of these colors, a final lead vocal was tracked, and, finally, extra percussion was inserted to add a dynamic to the piece. Effects added at the time of recording the instruments concerned, as opposed to adding them at the time of mixing. This was Caillat's preferred approach, and it indicates that, although the band may have written much of the material in the studio, the finished result was usually thought out and agreed upon before being recorded—once committed to analogue tape, an effect could not be removed.

Nicks's point of view as expressed in her lyrics—"Dreams" is a fine example, as is "I Don't Want to Know"—often contradicts Buckingham's apparent perspective of their relationship, as his songs suggest. Nicks has commented that, while she always tried to write a song that offered a conciliatory interpretation, she always felt that Buckingham went for the bitter alternative.

Maybe he did, but those bitter songs sure are pretty. "Never Going Back Again" was originally named "Brushes," a reference to the original drum track which featured Fleetwood playing brushes in a military snare pattern. The album version is stark and simple, Buckingham's lead vocal and a couple of guitars picked Leo Kottke style. The faintest trace of lush background vocals lurk behind Lindsey's peculiarly distant lead vocal, which contrasts so well with the relatively untreated acoustic guitars. It's a melodically uncluttered song with a simple chorus and a sharp resolve that says everything in a few elegant phrases.

The original demo version, which also included drums and electric guitar, was stripped down so the music matched the sentiment. The song was eventually redone in lengthy sessions at Sound City, recalls Morris and the guitars were slowed down a little to better accommodate the vocal. Collector's reissues of *Rumours* features the alternate "Brushes"

A slightly road-weary Fleetwood Mac: (left to right) John McVie, Lindsey Buckingham, Christine McVie, Stevie Nicks, Mick Fleetwood.

*Fleetwood Mac
during the peak of the
U.K. blues explosion:
(left to right)
Peter Green (front),
John McVie,
Jeremy Spencer,
Mick Fleetwood,
Danny Kirwan.*

*Into the mystic
with your host,
Peter Green.*

Peter Green and
Fleetwood Mac in
1968: (left to right)
John McVie,
Peter Green, Jeremy
Spencer (front),
Danny Kirwan,
Mick Fleetwood.

Fleetwood
Mac, 1976.

Christine McVie, taking a break from the Rumours treadmill in 1977.

A diaphanously pre-Goth Stevie Nicks.

Lindsey Buckingham with his post-Tusk haircut.

So you wanna be a rock 'n' roll star? John McVie in 1977.

Like punk never happened: Stevie Nicks and Mick Fleetwood meet their public in 1979.

Stevie calls it another lonely day.

Stuck in the middle with you: Mick Fleetwood often found himself in the role of mediator.

Fleetwood Mac celebrate at the L.A. Rock Awards, 1977.

The Royal Family of Soft Rock Fleetwood Mac in 1977: (left to right) John McVie, Christine McVie, Stevie Nicks, Mick Fleetwood, Lindsey Buckingham.

version with a solo electric guitar, an oddly picked thing with an e-bow phasing effect.

Outtakes of the song, which feature Buckingham's unmixed vocal up in the mix, clearly doubled and startlingly immediate, show the dramatic effect of shifting a song's focus (the final version has the acoustic guitar to the fore of the mix), even when there are only two instruments—voice and guitar. Most striking is the way that Buckingham throws all his being into the vocal: "Been down one time," he howls. The distant reverb and delay on the album's version makes one wonder if Buckingham was trying to hide his voice. Morris does not recall any particular efforts to mask Buckingham's lead vocal: "We did double everything, but everything in music is doubled [laughs]. Every vocal is doubled, tripled—since the Beatles, even Elvis had delay to double his voice." This comparison to Elvis is probably the key to Buckingham's recorded voice on much of his early work; the mysterious distance added to his vocals is reminiscent of the vocal sound heard on the old Sun Studio recordings that Buckingham so loved in his youth.

Caillat recalls that Buckingham was particularly uncomfortable on this song. He refused to let anyone hear his vocal until the guitar tracks were complete—only to find out that the vocal was in the wrong key. Cris Morris ponders some other explanations. "Maybe it wasn't a great recording; Lindsey was pretty hard on himself. We certainly didn't purposefully try and hide everything [with effects]. Maybe the vocals weren't as present as we wanted; a lot of the fidelity, I thought, was compromised between overdubbing, working on copies, and safeties and all that. Elton used to do that a lot—keep his vocal down in the track. Maybe Lindsey wanted to keep everything strong. The track is a little different sounding. It's a pretty simple track, but it took a long time; [laughs] the album took a year for 30 minutes worth of music, a lot of people working every day."

Fleetwood has commented that Christine McVie could have written "Don't Stop" 10 years before *Rumours*, but the difference is what he called "the cream"—the expansiveness of Buckingham's arrangement and the imaginative sonic palette that made this powerhouse shuffle into a shiny pop song. John Grissim remembers watching the band work on this song: "Fleetwood Mac was not a hard-driving rock band. This song represented a perfect confluence of Lindsey and Christine in melodic combination—that coming together of the melodic high end, and Christine's tremendous percussive ability: she could add to the bottom."

Ken Caillat says he found it difficult to get definition, what with all the instruments boogying along at the same time, but he did it, even making the bass kick through the din. A particular problem was dealing with the extra signal noise generated by Christine's classic "ice rink" Wurlitzer organ. Caillat told *The Penguin* that he would "nuke the top end and compensate with mids." In other words, his solution was to refocus the body of the sound on lower, fuller frequencies.

The song was written in a Sausalito condo as an encouragement to John McVie, although it was sung as an alternating duet by Buckingham and Christine McVie. Caillat and Dashut deliberately compressed and equalized the vocals of each singer so that they sound startlingly similar and delightfully ambiguous. Says Morris, "I remember her vocal mic—we used the same one on both, an AKG 414 mic. It has good high end, which is why they maybe sounded alike." Buckingham takes verse one; Christine McVie, verse two. They trade lines in the chorus and lapse into unison for the "yesterday's gone" and for the third verse. The keyboard, bass, and drums provide a fabulous heftiness to support the brief, squally guitar solo.

Another of Lindsey's little specialties shows up before the mass choir of the outro. It's a drum fill that doesn't resolve, but goes straight into a repeat of the chorus, and it is quite unnecessary but utterly wonderful. At the end, all the Plant employees, some dogs, and the band stood 'round a mic for the famous closing tag line.

The layout of the studio made for a little awkwardness when the band was laying down the foundation tracks. Cris Morris had to stand between Mick and Christine to keep time: "That [song] was recorded with Christine playing piano in a corner, a soundproofed-type area, so her back was to Mick. We put up a mirror so she could see Mick, who was facing her, but on the other side of the studio. I stood in the middle to help them kind of relate to each other. I kept time like a conductor. That's how that song started, and we had a big group in the end; everybody was in and out—it was spontaneous."

"Loving you, Isn't the right thing to do" from "Go Your Own Way" is surely one of the best first lines in rock music: simple, perfectly phrased, and with a great little twist that kicks stupid romance in the pants and breaks its choke hold on pop music. And it is certainly a line that could serve as the personal motto of every member of the band. "Go Your Own Way" is pure Buckingham genius, and it features a newwavey, half-strummed guitar, as well as the odd cycling of the guitar parts, which almost sound out of sync, until the chorus makes sense of the groove and locks everything in.

In the demo of the song, Buckingham tapped on Kleenex boxes—Fleetwood's drumming was his best attempt at copying this part, which was loosely based on the Rolling Stones' "Street Fighting Man." Fleetwood claims that his parts worked despite, or even because of, his "incompetence" (i.e. his inability to copy the beat). Using the console, Ken Caillat "played" Buckingham's guitar solo into the mix from six separate guitar takes. Of all his work on *Rumours*, Caillat is proudest of the guitar sounds, he told *The Penguin*. In order to keep things spontaneous, he had several different amps waiting in separate rooms, ready for action at any time.

Nicks, not surprisingly, hated the song but she was forced to sing it hundreds of times. The line about "packing up, shacking up," she claimed, was an unfair accusation. Singing it, she has said, is like going back in time to the same old arguments. As if that isn't bad enough, she told *Rolling Stone's* Daisann McLain in 1980, she had to strain to hit the high harmony. But it's that high harmony that puts the wild edge on the beautifully layered vocals in the chorus and cuts the song free.

With Christine McVie's tender "Songbird," there is a sudden lightening of the skies. The placement of this song after "Go Your Own Way" was most deliberate, Buckingham says; the intent was to contrast the male aggression displayed in that song with McVie's introspective femininity.

Ken Caillat overheard Christine messing around at the piano at the Record Plant and invited her to play it so he could get it on the two-track. The song had been written in a mere half an hour. Playing it made the rather private Mrs. McVie feel a little nervous and exposed. She has told John Grissim that she doesn't like to hear it too much, for those reasons. "It's a song and a prayer for everyone," she has said.

Ken Caillat realized that the song needed a recording venue as classy as the rendition in order to set the correct tone. His first choice was the Berkeley Community Theater, where he had previously recorded Joni Mitchell, but it was unavailable. The staff there recommended the Zellerbach Auditorium. An orchestral shell was installed, and for a touch of romance and drama, as a little gift to the singer, Caillat arranged for three simple spotlights and a dozen red roses. Christine was overwhelmed. The recording took place on March 3, 1976.

"That was another long day," laughs Cris Morris. "We tried various accompaniments on that. I remember, John McVie played a kind of fat bass, Lindsey played guitar, but we wound up dumping most of it. I think we kept a little of Lindsey's guitar; we had a lot of takes. The Zellerbach was empty. I remember it was a big deal; we had to pay these two union guys for sitting in the office—I think it cost $2,000, which was a lot back then—because it was a union hall and they had to pay the union to be there. That happens a lot in recording. The Record Plant was an independent studio; we used to do a lot of remote recordings—Oscars, Emmys. At the Zellerbach, we had a union engineer standing 'round. We had a remote truck, and I think we brought in a nine-foot Steinway piano. It was pretty much live, piano and vocal; she may have gone back to punch it up, as we did with 'Dreams.'"

There is a bootleg video in circulation that shows footage recorded onstage and offstage by the band during the *Rumours* tour of 1977. In one section, Christine McVie is interviewed about this song, and again, she appears to be uncomfortable talking about her deeper feelings. She talks about how it was Fleetwood's idea, to do "Songbird" as a stark finale to their show. Christine was "embarrassed" about singing it live, because of the song's emotional intimacy ("No, I won't tell you who it was written for—it's for everybody—the audience"). She stops, and in a moment that is typically Christine, she reaches down to fondle the patent leather shoes of the interviewer. And thus the conversation is sweetly and wordlessly ended.

Side two of *Rumours* opens with "The Chain." This began life as a song written by Christine called "Keep Me There." It had a bluesy, electric piano groove, which the rest of the band did not like. They almost tossed the whole song out—then they realized that there were parts they did like, such as the ending. It needed a bridge, so they cut one in. Of course, editing was not easy back in the analogue days of razor blades and ears. Buckingham decided they needed to do a reverse count from the parts they were keeping, in order to insert a meter to play to—in this case, Fleetwood's kick drum.

Cris Morris recalls the origins of the song: "It was [a combination of] two different songs, and as I recall, we weren't that thrilled with it. The choruses were then written, and they added those intro parts in L.A. The guitar, that was a track from Sausalito. Lindsey Buckingham did a lot of the other parts with Mick—the kick drum and guitar, the intro [verse] that goes throughout the song."

The song was left for some time without a vocal or any purposeful structure. After later reviewing the recording, the band decided they really liked the bridge, and Buckingham wrote verses around that melody. Stevie added lyrics that she had previously written for something else. Buckingham improvised a Dobro part, and the three songwriters all pooled their thoughts to come up with the indigo shadings of the folk-rock harmonies which open the song. It's McVie's bass that gives the song its life force, from the massive single note whooping in the chorus to the fierce intro-to-the-outro played on his Alembic fretless with the stainless steel fretboard.

"Mick had his style," says Morris. "John, it was hard for him to follow at times; most of the bass was redone on every song. He might have played initially, but he redid everything on every track. Mick Fleetwood is a stylized drummer; he has his own way of playing kick drum and it's not exact all the way through. It was easier for John to follow it after he heard it—this way, he got creative with bass parts." McVie would have liked the rest of the band to chime in sooner on his solo part, but luckily he was outvoted. In later years, in an interview in *The Sun* newspaper, Mick Fleetwood credited the authorship of the dominant riff in "The Chain" to John McVie. The writing credits for this song actually feature the entire band. It was a concept song in so many ways.

A constant comment heard in interviews conducted with the participants at these sessions concerns Buckingham's remarkable ability to retain an overview of an entire song, even when he was busy working on a song's minutia. It was this skill that brought the many fractured pieces of the song

"The Chain"[5] together. "The Chain" is the only example on this album of tracks that were recorded simultaneously being used together, just as they were recorded; in all other instances, the individual tracks were replaced by parts recorded at different times. The lone surviving pairing was that of the drums and guitar. Although the title "The Chain" may, in Buckingham's mind, have been a metaphor for the musical structure, the song went a lot deeper, to the heart of the band's experience and essence; the struggle to piece together that which, thereafter, could not be torn asunder.

"You Make Loving Fun" is a darkly groovy blues tune that was played on McVie's Hohner Clavinet, with a wah-wah pedal effect performed by Mick Fleetwood while lying on the floor. The verse begins in such a way that it appears to pick up from another song, with three perfectly placed words: "Sweeeeeeeet, wonderful you." No wonder this caused John McVie to admit to getting "a lump in my throat" the first time he heard the song, for Christine said it was written for her new boyfriend, the band's lighting director, Curry Grant. The finishing touches were added at Wally Heider, including the Beatlesesque hovering bridge that abruptly stops, then tips the listener right back into the groove. The sound of Christine's Fender Rhodes electric piano is also featured. Unlike some of the other

---

[5] A piece of Mac trivia from *The Penguin*: A fan wrote to Ken Caillat concerning a hidden Mac blooper at the beginning of "The Chain." If you listen very closely, says the fan, you can hear the sound of something being bumped, followed by a faint expletive, "f***!" Caillat confirms that this is true, if you listen to a mint copy of the original vinyl version, and that the offending moment was removed from the CD versions of the album.

compositions on the album, which took form during the recording, this song was complete in its demo form.

The Clavinet part accentuates Christine's great, rhythmic, left-hand technique. She considers herself part of the rhythm section, which is unusual for a keyboard player. She credits this approach to learning to play with John and Mick. This song was ultimately recorded in just that way, from the bass and drums upward. Ken Caillat comments that one of Christine's great strengths is the ability to add a counterpoint rhythm motif that sits back in the track and adds depth to the aural picture: this can be heard very well in this particular piece. Lindsey Buckingham has said that this is his favorite "Christine song" on the album. He made an effort to take her out of her usual textural paths with the keyboard arrangements, and the addition of the contrasting airy bridge section confirms this approach. Caillat believes the song to be as perfectly structured as any Cole Porter song.

John Grissim recalls watching Christine recording her parts in Sausalito: "Richard Dashut is a wonderful guy. The Record Plant had gotten these really cool airliner seats; you could sit back there, and I swear to God, when Stevie wasn't singing, she would sit there, cross-legged, crocheting, doing some stuff 'cause [that night] it was Christine's gig." Christine was recording, seated at the Steinway piano with a bottle of Blue Nun wine perched close at hand. "Dashut said to her, 'This is not a wine song, this is more of a cocaine song,' and Christine goes, 'Oh, well, I am *drunk.*' She might have been playing to the microphone, but the point was, it was an incredibly productive time for this band. They were a little overwhelmed—although Mick had been there before, so had

John—they knew something was happening. The first album had really established a strong connection, and they had no manager, so they were looking at an incredible situation."

The song "I Don't Want to Know" opens with a very unprepossessing, almost lumpen introduction, which of course, has a purpose, because when the song finally kicks in, its vibrant thrust is twice as powerful. Each time a verse launches out of the bridge, there is a huge infusion of energy. One of Nicks's country songs, it is brought to life by some great Buckingham-Nicks harmonies and Buckingham's strong country-pop guitar solo.

The original template for the song had a Buddy Holly/Everly Brothers feel, which isn't immediately apparent on the recorded version but which would be the reason this song sounds so oddly perky. Not surprisingly, the song was originally written in the days of Buckingham Nicks, and it was therefore, presumably, turned down by others.

Mick Fleetwood has commented that the song illustrates perfectly what Nicks and Buckingham brought to the band, and what he saw in them in the first place. Buckingham Nicks always had the harmonies; however, this song sounds much poppier than anything on their debut solo album—it's concise and punchy. Buckingham acknowledges that it's the odd song out on *Rumours*; it was chosen because it was so straightforward, and because it was just what they needed at the time of sequencing the album for a vinyl LP format.

The song was recorded in just three hours at Wally Heider's Studio 4, and according to Ken Caillat, the atmosphere between the two vocalists was extremely frosty that day. With no Christine to leaven the harmonies, it was just the two of them, but like true professionals, they worked together with energy and precision, and with no hint of animosity. The instrumental accompaniment to the vocals is comparatively slight. The piano is a jaunty, simple, plodding accompaniment, but magic appears in the way the guitar builds momentum, almost pouncing at the beginning of each new verse, bringing a burst of verve and energy. "I Don't Want to Know" was the song that replaced the longer, now legendary "Silver Springs" on the finished album, and suffers, unfairly, from being written off as an interloper by many Fleetwood Mac devotees.

The mournful, beautiful "Oh Daddy"[6] is Christine McVie's best vocal effort in several albums, a thoughtful, sexy, old English version of the Stones' "Fool To Cry." The bass is uncharacteristically busy, for John McVie, at least— and can the listener possibly get enough of Mick Fleetwood's fabulous punchy, papery snare? This song should be a set piece for would-be vocal arrangers: the lightest golden weave of harmony and counterpoint from Buckingham and Nicks complements the midnight musings dedicated to Mick Fleetwood. Christine admits to some deliberate sarcasm in the line which asks why "Daddy" is so right when she's so wrong. Nicks, she says, gave her the last line of the chorus. The choice of words to harmonize is impeccable. Stevie chimes in on the last syllable of the word "around," elongating the vowel and then letting it go, like a ribbon that ripples to the ground.

---

[6] Caillat humorously notes that the flaking of the tape following the overdub abuse almost changed the title of this song to "Oh Addy."

"Oh, yes, that's a great song," enthuses Morris. "It was one of those piano tuner songs; one of the criteria in those days was to start with a really good piano sound. This one was recorded in Sausalito." Fanatics will listen for the little keyboard blip at the end, hidden in the semi-random keyboard figures that curtail the song. It wasn't part of the song, says Lindsey Buckingham, it was just Christine trying to get the attention of the control room, but they left it in anyway.

"What was remarkable about 'Gold Dust Woman,'" says John Grissim, "is Stevie's voice was so sure—she's got this husky kind of gin voice that guys just *go* for. It's reminiscent of Brenda Lee's voice; people always used to say of her that she sang below the belt, and Stevie had some of that. Here's this small woman with this hoarse voice, sensual—she was learning with "Rhiannon"—by now she knew how to pitch and do it properly. What the Record Plant gave her was that freedom, that power to use the studio as an instrument ... Stevie Nicks, she just drove that song."

"I think we're talking 20 or 30 takes on this," says Morris. "Everybody was pretty critical in those days. We all kind of produced, everybody had a say—what was good, what wasn't [laughs]. It was a group effort, and Stevie worked hard. Her little poodle, Ginny, used to hang out under the seats." Stevie began recording "Gold Dust Woman" standing in a brightly lit room, which was dimmed little by little, until she was cocooned in the gloom, wrapped in a shawl and perched on a chair, Red Riding Hood's grandma. Of course she was surrounded by her usual stash; Grissim identified Kleenex, a Vicks inhaler, and Calistoga mineral water. "Onstage, she's the goddess of whatever," said Christine to John Grissim, after one of their shows, "but offstage she's very often like a little old lady with a cold." The song is Nicks's take on herself, the Mystical Rocker, and about her life in Los Angeles. No mention of Kleenex or bunions.

According to Buckingham, the song was recorded with a looser, jazzier approach, and in this case, it was the right way. His overdubs were added several months down the line, after McVie had added his final bass part to Fleetwood's larger-than-life boomy tom tom and Christine's rhythmic Fender Rhodes. The sounds of breaking glass and marauding animals were added after the song was completed, a disappointment to those who thought it might have been the band having one of their studio fights. The band's roadies were sent out to find six panes of glass, which Fleetwood proceeded to break in the isolation booth of Studio D at the Village Recorder.

"Silver Springs" was not included on the original vinyl version of the album, but it surfaced on the CD version in edited form. Lindsey Buckingham said that he was most pleased with the contrasting layers and textures of the guitars on this song.

Nicks hoped that this epic "ballad of Stevie and Lindsey" would be on the radio to follow Buckingham forever— something to remind him of the falling out of love, and what could have been. It ended up as the B-side to "Go Your Own Way" (oh, bitter irony!). Inspired by a road sign pointing to Silver Spring, Maryland, it is a meandering southern rock ballad, anguished and intense.

Mick the mediator was the unfortunate soul who had to break the news to Nicks that the song would not appear on the album. He chose the Record Plant parking lot as the venue for delivering this disappointing news. Nicks kicked up quite a fuss at the time, but as Caillat told *The Penguin*, Nicks was very aware of her options, and she chose wisely. The vinyl album format meant that only a finite amount of music could be included, and, at over six minutes, the full-length version of "Silver Springs" would have had to be aggressively edited to fit. Nicks had a three-song limit to work with, and she ended up substituting "I Don't Want to Know."

The band also worked on another Nicks song that didn't make the final three. Her "Think About It," a gritty, electric country rocker with Buckingham's raunchy rhythmic guitars driving the medium-paced number, was half recorded when the band realized it wouldn't be included and set it aside. As Caillat noted in the online pages of *The Penguin*, band members often found themselves with a lot of spare time, and Nicks would often retire to another room to write and record new ideas. "That's Alright" was another Nicks composition that was pulled from consideration during the *Rumours* sessions.

Caillat also revealed that Nicks's song lyrics were routinely edited—not for offensive content, but to shorten them. Stevie Nicks, interviewed by Richard Dashut for the *Rumours* DVD release, showed that she viewed this editing process as a necessary part of the artistic whole. "Nobody would want to hear those songs go on and on—not even me," she chuckled, in typically candid Nicks style.

Only the best songs, said Caillat, made it through to the final sequencing—there was no political maneuvering, no cosseting of hurt feelings. Ideas, he said, were listened to in "a cooperative atmosphere," although Buckingham, in recognition of his ability to visualize the bigger musical picture, would have the casting vote if they came to an impasse. Each song, no matter how simple, was given the same amount of love, said Caillat, although songs like "Silver Springs," with their many colors, may have taken a little more time.

Caillat also pointed out that there were no decisions made in the name of avoiding conflict. After all, there was already enough of that—what was a little more? Throughout it all, the band still managed to salvage moments of harmony in their workplace. They would go out to local restaurants, and, while they may have split into groups, they did not actively avoid each other.

Indeed, the sequencing of the songs on the album is very democratic—no one songwriter gets two consecutive songs, although side one is really the Lindsey Buckingham show. His three songs, each describing varying shades of anger and disillusion, intersperse the gentler works of Nicks and Christine. Nicks's "Dreams" tells the other side of the bitter story recounted in "Second Hand News" and Buckingham deliberately chose the tender "Songbird" to follow the bitter bluster of "Go Your Own Way."

"The Chain" is the only song written by the entire band, and it is in many ways the band's manifesto. A more obvious placement for it would have been as the album's closer, but instead, it opens side two. Both sides of the collection begin with a powerful blast of energy. Placed as the opening song of side two, "The Chain" serves to summarize the story so far, and it also provides contrast to the tone of "Songbird." The listener is constantly shifted from one mood to another, following the band on their emotional roller coaster.

The remaining songs are those of Nicks and Christine McVie. The jaunty "You Make Loving Fun" follows the heavy vibrations of "The Chain," and, just in case the listener had forgotten, the old-fashioned country style harmonies of "I Don't Want to Know" bring back the central theme of splintered relationships. Again, one of Christine's songs ("Oh Daddy") is used to sweeten the pain, before the album closes with a song that defined the rock culture of the day, "Gold Dust Woman." Thus the album closes on a rather open-ended piece—a study of a person rather than of a finite relationship. The very ungolden sound effects—the breaking glass and bizarro noises—also point toward the shapes that *Tusk* would assume, although maybe only Buckingham knew this at the time.

Caillat reflected that, although Fleetwood told Dashut and Caillat they were producers early on in Sausalito, they still had to prove themselves as such. The album credits had still to be written. Caillat and Dashut can take great credit for the album seeing the light of day, as a result of both their creative input and their empathetic ability to keep the band focused, while still being sensitive to their pain; they were able to keep the group grounded. All of the band felt comfortable with Dashut, who was able to soak up the angst and keep smiling.

For his part, Caillat was able to translate the band's ideas within the restrictive parameters of audio recording. Sometimes, he recalled, he would have a problem getting both the keyboards and the guitars to sit comfortably in a stereo field, without battling each other. He realized that a frequent problem was that the two instruments would be playing in the same octave. To solve this, he would ask one of the players to redo his or her part, moving it up or down a third, so as to add contrast, rather than busyness.

This potential for sonic conflict was acknowledged by Buckingham. He has commented that, upon joining the band, he had to significantly rework the way he played guitar in order to find space between the two McVies. John's bass playing, he has said, is unusually melodic, and the keyboards, by their very nature, tend to take up a lot of aural space.

By the late fall of 1976, as the mixing was drawing to a close, Warner Brothers was extremely eager to finally hear the band's labor of great love. In the January 1978 issue of *Rolling Stone*, writer Dave Marsh mused that the only reason the label wasn't totally panicked into breaking down the door to the mixing room (they had now been waiting 11 months) was because the band's previous album was still selling in substantial quantities.

Finally, the album had a name. One day around November, John McVie, who was all too aware of the various tall tales generated by the band's complicated lives, put down his bass and came up with the album's spot-on title: *Rumours*. McVie rarely spoke up, but when he did, people listened. In talking to Cameron Crowe in a *Rolling Stone* feature, 1977, McVie explained his apparently taciturn nature, saying he would certainly say something if he felt it was of great importance. It's just that most times, there's nothing to say. In the meantime, he just played bass, because that's what he did. By December 1976 the band had finally started sequencing the album and Warner Brothers released the first single from the album. "Go Your Own Way" was an instant success, and it reached Number 10 in the *Billboard Hot 100* charts.

The cover of *Rumours* is a continuation of the theme established on its predecessor, *Fleetwood Mac*. It features a stark, black-and-white depiction of professional beanstalk Mick Fleetwood, dressed in his Renaissance best. This time, instead of the kneeling John McVie, we see Stevie Nicks, poised in a graceful and tastefully risqué ballet pose. The album was designed by Desmond Strobel using a concept devised by the band and photographer Herbert Worthington III. Worthington had worked with the band on both *Fleetwood Mac* and *Heroes Are Hard to Find*.

Stevie Nicks had bad memories of the cover shoot for the Buckingham Nicks LP. She recalled spending her last $111 on a sexy blouse, which she hoped would knock the stylists off their feet. She was crushed when she was asked to remove the blouse so the twosome could be photographed with bare shoulders and more. She told *Us* magazine in 1990 that she had been determined not to go for the obvious skin shot for the *Rumours* cover, but to do the exact opposite: she was going to make herself look both sexy and mysterious under 18 pounds of chiffon, lace, and velvet. It would be this mystique that would keep her distinct, she decided. She had always loved long, flowing, romantic clothes, and she took these ideas to her designer, Margi Kent. "We did clothes for everything," recalls Kent. "We never knew what was going to be used. Herbie had this concept that no one got at the time, but it ended up being a real trademark for Fleetwood Mac. After that [cover] she started using that kind of look in several colors; she didn't only wear black!" And indeed, the same look reappeared in white instead of black—on the cover of Nicks's debut solo album, *Bella Donna*.

The only unusual aspect of Nicks's costume on the cover of *Rumours* is her footwear; she is wearing ballet shoes instead of her signature platform boots. "Oh, those boots," recalls Kent. "We girls had all gotten these great platform boots. Then she decided she could probably wear them onstage. They were pretty tall, but they looked so beautiful and cool. We had a pair specifically made for her. She had Maya shoe design do her boots; we sent them all the swatches. They did powder pink, cream—oh the cream! When she wore that onstage, it was unbelievable, because the lighting director could change the [shading] so dramatically, as opposed to black; you can't change that much. She went to the same boot maker until he retired. We get calls all the time at the studio: 'Where does Stevie get her boots?'"

Worthington had stayed with the band in one of the houses in Mill Valley during the Sausalito sessions, and much of the album's jacket photography is from that time. It's all very whimsical, very sunny and spontaneous stuff, and is much removed from the archly posed and conceived cover. In the various shots are all the crew members, including John Courage. A group shot of all associated with the band includes the unmistakable presence of Bob Welch, wearing a beret and pair of glasses that would have given Elton John pause for thought. A candid shot of Nicks whispering in Christine McVie's ear establishes a theme that is echoed on the other side of the montage insert, which features an illustration of two penguins, one whispering in the ear of the other. This side is dominated by a casual shot of the band, again relaxed and tan. Carefully placed at their lounging feet is one of the album's costars, a bottle of Blue Nun wine.

During the shoot, Worthington recalled in an interview for the DVD rerelease of *Rumours*, there was a lot of spontaneous fun with the band, which ended up as a montage of shots on the album's inner insert. He was photographing Stevie and Christine one night when John joined in. Improvising with a wine bottle, a guitar lead, and a mic stand, he created a tableau of himself receiving an alcohol IV drip. It was John's way of expressing the *Rumours* agony without getting too serious, for he did not write lyrics. The finished result can be seen as the third photo down on the far right of the photo montage.

The photo sequence on the back of the album sleeve came about in a similar way. The back theme is the opposite of the intricately staged front cover image. Above the main photo of the band, looking relaxed and Californian, is a sequence showing, in frame one, John McVie approaching Lindsey Buckingham, and catching his attention. This was unrehearsed, says Worthington. The friction between McVie and Buckingham has been acknowledged by the band, and the subtext of the photo is, "What was McVie going to do to Buckingham?" Frame two shows John smiling intently and mischievously at the camera, while Lindsey and Christine share a comment of their own. In the final frame McVie hugs Buckingham. The two women hug each other. Mick is left alone to the right, the lone mediator and pensive sage.

Listening to this album, to the five people playing and singing their hearts out to (and often at) one another, one comes away with a feeling that the music must have *really* mattered for them to set aside their differences and to sing harmony on insults directed at themselves. This was a modern-day opera, and the listening public had heard enough gossip to be able to construct its own version of the story behind the songs. Who would have believed that these were the former beer warriors of Benifold?

Warner Brothers was so delighted with what they heard that they took out an ad in the March issue of *Rolling Stone* which featured Cameron Crowe's cover story on the band, declaring that the label would be pressing and shipping the album in platinum-selling quantities. "Ready on your end?" the ad asked the readers.

platinum misery

In the bicentennial summer of 1976, it was ironic that some of the best-selling artists in the United States, outside of the new and monstrous disco boom, were U.K. expats from the bluesy 1960s: Rod Stewart, Fleetwood Mac, and former Humble Pie guitarist Peter Frampton. These were truly the golden years of rock: everybody loved music, and they gave up their money to prove it. The scale of the rock machinery expanded; advances in sound reinforcement and planning meant that stadium- and arena-sized venues were the new theaters for this generation.

"The mid 1970s were a time when promoters began to understand how to mount large-scale concerts and major tours," says former *Rolling Stone* editor Ben Fong-Torres. "It began around '73, '74, with major bands like Dylan and the Stones. Later, Fleetwood Mac was the perfect band to do that, to fill an arena with the right presence and presentation. The Bill Grahams of the day were really getting going, mounting major concert tours. There was a lot of money about."

This resulted in a craze for releasing live albums— *Frampton Comes Alive* sold an unprecedented eight million albums in 1976 alone. For years, Warner Brothers encouraged the band to release such an album, and for years the band resisted, preferring to offer original studio material.

That summer, in a break from recording *Rumours*, the band toured for six weeks, playing in front of tens of thousands of people, in the company of the Eagles and Jefferson Starship.

One concert, titled, "A Day on the Green," was put together by the influential San Francisco promoter Bill Graham, and staged at the Oakland Coliseum in front of 60,000 people. It featured the day's best-selling performers: Peter Frampton, Gary Wright, and Fleetwood Mac. Fleetwood Mac and Frampton had played the event the previous year. *Fleetwood Mac* was still climbing the charts, and the thousands who saw the band play in 1976 were reminded just how much the next album was worth waiting for. All skepticism regarding Nicks's rock credibility had evaporated; she was now the most visible female in rock music. The concert marked a new dawn after the pain of the days at Sausalito; relations among the band's members improved somewhat, and Mick and Jenny, though divorced, began to live together again.[7]

During their tour to promote *Fleetwood Mac* the previous summer, just before the big-time album sales, the band was not always treated with politeness by the acts they were supporting. "Get those broads offstage," was a phrase Mick Fleetwood remembers hearing from stage management staff on more than one occasion. Fleetwood Mac and its crew treated their own supporting acts with much more courtesy, remembers Michael Freeman, who worked with Fleetwood Mac while serving as tour manager to one of their support acts. "They were gracious. It was a huge stage; there was plenty of room for our gear. They were very cordial and very helpful."

---

[7] They would soon have to remarry to give Jenny and their children legal resident status, after Mick and the other Britons in the band finally qualified for their green cards.

Backstage after their fall 1976 concert in San Diego, John Grissim, writing for *Crawdaddy*, painted a picture of mild-mannered but widespread adulation from the hordes of fans hoping for a brief audience with the band. In the back of a limousine, heading to the hotel, Stevie Nicks spoke excitedly of Fleetwood's fast-developing showmanship, and she wished that Buckingham had a little more room in the arrangements to expand his solos, now that he was on top of his game.

"My purpose was to capture the emotional landscape. If you could read between the lines after that San Diego concert—and it's just me and Stevie in the back of that long limousine—I was thinking, 'I might just get lucky ...,'" he laughed. "It was an exciting time; driving down the San Diego Freeway after the concert, to the Mission Island Travelodge, the sodium vapor lights with their salmon pink, every-three-seconds light across Stevie Nicks's face, a little bit of that gold dust and glitter on her nose and the perspiration on her brow ... Stevie wasn't a roue or anything, and I was always a gentleman, but Stevie obviously knew, it was clear." Nothing happened. Grissim should never have called her "Sheila" that time in the Record Plant kitchen.

Grissim traveled with the band later that summer when they played triumphant homecoming shows in southern California. He found Buckingham, now 26, living in a white stucco home with Richard Dashut and Bob Aguirre, Buckingham's old Fritz bandmate. Buckingham had stepped out of the darkness following his split with Nicks and was surprised to find himself optimistic about the future. He commented to Grissim that Nicks's new romantic relationship with Eagle Don Henley was "good for her."

This was definitely a move in the right direction for Buckingham's state of mind, and it contrasts with a scene from earlier in the summer, which was recounted by Stevie Nicks to Courtney Love in a 1997 interview for *Rolling Stone*. In 1976 Fleetwood Mac and the Eagles found themselves recording at the same studio in Miami, just when Don Henley had begun his courtship of Nicks. One day, to Nicks's dismay, Henley sent over a limousine full of gifts—a stereo, records, fruit, and flowers—which were delivered in full view of the band. This display of courtly extravagance in the hotel breakfast room was apparently not well received by Buckingham. As the driver unloaded the bounty, Nicks attempted to deflect the delivery. Nicks may have been elevated to the role of rock princess, but she wasn't always at ease with the lavish adulation it sometimes brought.

Despite his new fame and fortune, Buckingham had yet to feel validated. As he told John Grissim in late 1976, being in the limelight caused him to question himself, rather than sail ahead with blithe confidence. "Some of these moments were very incandescent," says Grissim. "I [went] to spend some time with Lindsey; he was living in L.A. I told him, 'Man, you are now a bona fide rock star. You are part of the aristocracy, and you need to dig it a little bit.' He said, 'What do you mean?' 'Well, let's go to the Rainbow on Sunset Strip and check it out. Come on, man, let's just go—it'll be fun.' I picked him up. He was still a little naive in a way. I wasn't mentoring him, but in a way I was part of the bullshit rock 'n' roll establishment, [so I could say] 'Here's where ya go ...'

"We went to the Rainbow, the hip place of the time, and sure enough, two guys from REO Speedwagon came over, and there were terrific, smashing-looking women who discreetly swarmed the table; it was very quietly and tastefully done. They didn't know who he was, and I said [assumes tone of velvet discretion], 'Lindsey Buckingham!'—and the word spread. I think it was in the women's room within 30 seconds. It was a hoot to watch. I said, 'This is it.' I was half joking and half serious—'This is *the* S-C-E-N-E; the world is your oyster.' And he kind of like—he was a sweet guy—and anyway, neither of us got in any trouble whatsoever—much to my chagrin! I realize that from a career standpoint, that I was Tonto with the Lone Ranger; you never got the girl, but you sure got to look hard!"

This time, Warner Brothers had planned an extravagant party for the band's L.A. homecoming. At their show at the Universal Amphitheater that fall, they played to a devoted and high-profile crowd, which included Iranian royalty and Elton John. Of course they couldn't rest long on their laurels, because they were still working on the album, this time in a small studio across the street from the amphitheater. Mixing *Rumours* at the Producer's Workshop in Los Angeles, Lindsey Buckingham met his soon-to-be new love, Carol Ann Harris, a young woman from Tulsa, Oklahoma, who was working as the studio receptionist. Harris was to be his close companion for the next six years.

While the band had been suffering for its art in Sausalito, recording the greatest soft rock album ever, a counterculture had been born and was growing up fast. This love child of 1960s garage rock and 1970s art rock was philosophically opposed to the airbrushed sound of Los Angeles and the extravagant budgets that went with it. Squalling punk rock bands were rudely awakening the youth of both the United Kingdom and the United States by preaching their gospel of crude brevity. It would take a good year before the music registered in the mainstream, and although it did nothing to break the cresting wave of Fleetwood Mac's golden years, it would have a profound effect, a couple of years down the line, on the album that followed *Rumours*.

The domination of disco was also another story. The genre was about to enter its third triumphant year on the national charts, and it appeared to be taking over the nation's nightlife, as small music venues converted to dance clubs, complete with garish flashing lights and DJ booths. But disco could not elbow aside the gilded princes of rock. The record that came to symbolize all that was West Coast and decadent had only just been released. The Eagles' *Hotel California* was recorded in the same time period as *Rumours*, and it hit the Number One position in the U.S. charts in January 1977. It spoke of emptiness in paradise, of the acknowledgment that there was a price to pay for those gilded lifestyles—and of the bill that was coming due. *Rumours* was released in the United States on February 4, 1977. It was the yin to *Hotel California*'s yang; instead of glamorous ennui and cerebral guitar solos, it was all heart, passion, and pain.

The *Rolling Stone* cover of March 1977 was photographed by Annie Leibowitz, and it shows the band in a big bed together. Amid a lot of bare feet and smooshy hair, Mick and Stevie are hugging happily, Christine and Lindsey are snuggled together at the opposite end of the bed, looking a little detached, and John McVie is off to the side, reading a girlie magazine. After the photo shoot, Buckingham told VH1, he and Nicks lay on the bed for about an hour, hugging. After the past 12 months of acrimony, this show of love apparently "freaked everybody out."

Rumours, noted writer Dave Marsh in *Rolling Stone*, sold enough copies at the height of its success to go gold twice a month. Marsh also pointed out that the Recording Industry Association of America had, in 1975, increased the gold standard for record sales to half a million copies, in response to the industry-wide increase in retail sales. Within a year of its release in February 1977, *Rumours* had sold over 8 million copies, and it showed little sign of losing momentum.

This was partly due to a rich harvest of chart singles. Following the previous year's release of "Go Your Own Way," "Dreams" (backed by "Songbird") was released on March 24, 1977, and gave the band its first Number One single. "Don't Stop," backed by "Never Going Back Again," came out July 6, 1977 and reached Number Three. Finally, "You Make Loving Fun," coupled with "Gold Dust Woman," was released on October 5, 1977, and reached Number Five in the *Billboard* charts. *Rumours* itself reached Number One in the U.S. album charts in April 1977 and stayed there for six months. Over in the United Kingdom, it reached Number One in the album charts in January 1978. By the end of 1978, Fleetwood Mac had swept just about every award in rock music.

The album was released into a market that had been primed by the gossip columns. Fans vibrated with overworked expectations, and were consequently quite ready for the first hint of disappointment. Many had come to believe the album would never be finished and few thought the band would stay together long enough to actually promote *Rumours* with a tour. It would have been a prime opportunity for the rock press to do some hype-deflating showboating, but this didn't happen. The critics mostly liked what they heard, although *Creem*'s Stephen Demorest found only "Dreams" to be truly magical; in the review, he admits to having a crush on Nicks. Of course, the critics noted the astounding amount of press inches that had been devoted to the band in the previous 18 months, but *Crawdaddy*'s Samuel Graham went so far as to suggest that the high drama that took place during the recording of *Rumours* had actually made the music stronger, and he affirmed the fine group effort of the whole album, especially in light of the band's crumbling relationships.

Several reviews mentioned increased respect for Lindsey Buckingham's work—the release of "Go Your Own Way" in late 1976 had been a fine way to define the album. There would be few pop fans who would have missed the message in that song. "If you're not hooked now," wrote the wild and wiggy Fred Schuers in *Circus* magazine, "better check your pulse." Samuel Graham reported in *Crawdaddy* that he felt that Buckingham really "came into his own" in this album. Several reviewers were impressed by Buckinham's acoustic work, as by the varied textures of his electric guitar work.

As usual, everybody—except for Demorest—loved Christine McVie's contributions. Unlike Buckingham and Nicks, her retiring stage persona, vocal style, and mellifluous timbre did not seek attention. Both *Rolling Stone* and *Crawdaddy* praised "Songbird" as a sincere gesture of peace and love in a swirling sea of rancor and ruffled emotions. Similarly, they recognized "You Make Loving Fun" for being a celebration of the new, as opposed to a postmortem on the old. Interestingly, the angelic vocal interplay in the song's bridge was singled out as a favorite part by several reviewers.

Unlike *Creem*'s Demorest, John Swenson, writing for *Rolling Stone*, did not feel that Stevie Nicks had anything on the album that compared to "Rhiannon," and he diagnosed "Dreams" as suffering from a rather nasal vocal. This did not bother the purchasing public, who sent the single to Number One. Despite this minor criticism, the consensus was that the vocal teamwork, as well as the years of experience brought to the project by Fleetwood and the McVies, gave the album both fire and integrity—qualities that outshined the gaudy neon of the album's prepublicity. The band, all agreed, was making musical progress, not treading water and pandering to commercial expectations.

Fleetwood Mac was now the equal of the Eagles in terms of both songwriting and performance. Demorest insisted they were actually *better* than the Eagles, thanks to the edge provided by the "rustic authenticity" of Buckingham and Nicks' rootsy folk blues. Swenson, in *Rolling Stone*, made the point that vocal harmonies were the key feature of the West Coast sound, and that Fleetwood Mac was now "one of the genre's main proponents."

Swenson also noted that Fleetwood Mac's alchemic transformation from lead to gold, from British blues group to Southern California folk-pop band, was not such a long stretch after all. The British version of the blues revival, he pointed out, embraced rural American folk music as much as it did urban blues; seen in this light, Christine McVie's vocal similarity to English folk-rock singer Sandy Denny, rather than to any of the British blues shouters, makes perfect sense.

In his autobiography, Mick Fleetwood asserts that the winning sound of *Rumours* was no creative accident. He says that Richard Dashut and Lindsey Buckingham, who shared a house together, spent long hours listening to such masters of record making as the Beach Boys, analyzing the structure and sound of the pop masterpieces. Their work was not in vain; audio expert Chris Johnson has analyzed the sonogram produced by Fleetwood's kick drum sound on the album and has pronounced it absolutely perfect in every way. Of course, people who fell in love with the album via tinny car radios may not have appreciated this, but it goes to show that *Rumours* had something for everyone.

Cris Morris had worked with rhythm-and-blues legend Tower of Power, which he thought was the best band in the world at one point; its musicianship and musicality was unparalleled, yet the band never really connected with the wider public in the same way that it impressed their fellow musicians. Most record buyers did not listen with a musician's ear, and it was difficult for music business insiders to set aside their own taste and opinions and predict what would or would not be a widespread success. Says Morris, "You never know—but with *Rumours*, we knew! In our minds we knew it had to be a hit. We were high from the success of the previous singles, and the tracks were pretty good; you knew it had to be good, or you were dead. We willed it!

"We all thought it was flawed as far as sound quality was concerned; you're schlepping tapes around for a year. We kept at it, and when it came out, we knew the songs were good. The emotion was all there, and a lot of rock 'n' roll is just being able to capture the emotion. That stayed there; that was still on the tapes, but the fidelity [laughs], I don't know. It got good reviews, though, for fidelity, and sometimes you believe the public though you may not think so yourself. It sounded good on small speakers, sounded good in the car—and that is a lot of the key! It was up for a Grammy for sound, so...."

Of course, there were always naysayers. Ken Caillat told *The Penguin* that one of his friends heard the album and regretfully told him that he heard *no* hits. Not one. Caillat charitably keeps the person's identity to himself, despite having been quite disheartened by this pronouncement at the time. Caillat soon came around. He remembers the day he knew the album was big; he turned on his car radio to hear a DJ crowing about the "fabulous new Fleetwood Mac album." On came "Go Your Own Way," and Caillat heard, with fresh ears, just how good it was. The anonymous friend, one hopes, learned to enjoy the taste of humble pie, for it would have been on the menu for a mighty long time.

when music mattered

It is quite rare that such anticipation, of both an artistic and a commercial jackpot, is rewarded so abundantly. Writing in *Rolling Stone* in 1978, Dave Marsh attempted to find out why *Rumours* did so phenomenally well. He quizzed many of the executives at Warner Brothers but could not find anyone who admitted doing anything extraordinary for the release of the record, except, as their print ads in the music press boasted, making it available in huge numbers. A TV and movie theater ad, which ran at the time of *Rumours's* release, shows some cartoon penguins skating on a pond. It is certainly more whimsical than the hard sell of sex and glamour one might have expected, and it supports the assertion of Warner Brothers executive Derek Taylor that nothing unusual was done to pitch the product.

Maybe nothing unusual was undertaken[8] in the way of gimmicks or specialized marketing, but the promotional push was certainly proportional to the label's expectations. All hands were summoned on deck, according to Mickey Shapiro. "Most of the marketing setup was a very coordinated effort by both the Warner Brothers marketing [sales and promotion] teams, along with a very complete plan created by WEA [the distribution company]. The two teams worked *very* well.

---

8 The promotional effort for *Tusk* was much more lavish (see chapter 12, Tusk!) even though the executives pushing *Tusk* did not have the optimism they had for *Rumours*.

"I did attend some of these planning meetings. I think that *everyone* realized that, after the first Fleetwood Mac record with Stevie and Lindsey, *Rumours* could go all the way. The PAP [promotion, advertising, and publicity] budgets were very large. It must be remembered that the buzz had a full year to develop, as the record took so long to get done. The company had bits and pieces and knew what they had. Mo Ostin, Joe Smith, Lou Dennis, Stan Cornyn, Russ Thyrett— *all* of them know what was coming and opened their wallets accordingly. And remember, this was all pre MTV!"

The band was fortunate to be dealing with the best record company around, according to many in the industry. Says Ben Fong-Torres, "Warner Brothers had a very strong presence and power in the industry—the label itself was such a major brand that anybody who was on it had an advantage right away. They had the benefit of Stan Cornyn in the creative services department. He created this hip veneer, this sense of humor—a self-effacing kind of thing that connected with the music's audience. He created this brand, long before branding was known outside of advertising, and it just clicked in a way no other label could. Other labels like Columbia tried to emulate that attitude and even the look of some of the attitude."

Mickey Shapiro notes that there was a growth in business strategizing, which put in place machinery big enough to serve anyone who came to buy: "I think that marketing techniques became exponentially improved with the use of mass merchants. Tower [Records] and Best Buy—particularly Tower—developed methods of stacking up records on the floor; for those days, revolutionary techniques of marketing."

The release of *Rumours* happened at an auspicious point in record business history. The album benefited from the new: a larger-scale commercial network and the improved integration of marketing and distribution. "The guy who worked there in those days, he's since passed on, his name was Bob Regehr; they had this department devoted to assisting the artists," says Shapiro. "If an artist was on tour, they made sure that the records came to the store, that the radio people came to the tour. There was a quantum leap in the understanding of the relationship between records and radio and retail.

"Secondly, the distribution networks themselves, in particular WEA—the distribution network of Warners, Elektra, and Atlantic—became brilliant. The record labels and the distribution had parallel departments. It was run like it was a great relay race. You could literally have records on radio and in retail shops on the same day—and if you look at the geography of this country, that was an amazing exercise."

Rumours also benefited from the old: the experience of the personnel, the affluence of the industry (although the clock was ticking), and the willingness to support art for art's sake—because at this time, the record companies could afford to indulge their artists. "There was an expertise in leadership—at Warners we had Mo Ostin and his team. The people in marketing would interface very well with the WEA folks, like the relationship between a doctor and a hospital," says Shapiro.

It also helped that back in 1976, rock music was the nation's primary youth culture. Says Michael Freeman, "Music was a priority in young people's lives. It's not right now—it's a blend of the visual, audio, and game arts. In the

1970s, everybody was going to a club or concert three nights a week—they wanted nothing but music! The economics are so different now."

Rumours is an excellent album, but it also benefited from the momentum of forces other than the band's creativity. Their music—and their personal history—was a perfect blend of AM pop radio fare and FM underground. This genre of soft rock came to be known as AOR (album-oriented rock) or MOR (middle of the road, the more dismissive description of the two).

Ben Fong-Torres, who wrote *The Hits Just Keep on Coming*, a detailed and passionate history of U.S. Top 40 radio, recalls the obscure beginnings in the United States of FM radio, the format that came to define the charts of the mid-1970s. "FM radio started to sell records in the early 1970s. Until then, it was really unknown on that level, pop music. The first stations that tried to do it were mostly playing music called 'MOR,' or 'beautiful music,' or 'audiophile'—taken from jazz and classical genres. In terms of rock culture, when the first underground stations came along, they drew a very active audience of these young people who were part of the hip culture and didn't have anybody else talking to them. So if you wanted to sell certain items [laughs]—waterbeds, back-packs, smoking paraphernalia, or news about concerts and albums—that was where you went.

"The mainstreaming of FM really didn't take place for a few more years, as the word and music spread and the corporations began to take notice of what was happening and converted their stations to a format, either free-form or similar to free-form. For a number of years early on, in the late 1960s, people simply did not have FM radio; they had heard about the underground stations but didn't necessarily have access to it, so they had to make do with AM."

Fleetwood Mac's blend of free-form FM rock and AM pop bridged the gap between the two previously separate formats. "Harmonies weren't particularly interesting in those days; it was considered too pop," says Shapiro. "In those days, there was a dividing line—are you an underground group or are you AM pop? Fleetwood Mac seemed to transcend it. If you analyze their music carefully, it was pretty much pop radio, but it was played from their really deep roots and their blues background. Of course, radio mattered, but I believe the real driver at this time was this, from my perspective—that enormous live audience reaction to them."

Ed Rosenblatt, then the sales and promotions chief at Warner Brothers, offered a simple reason for the album's massive success. He claimed that there had been a huge increase in retail outlets, and that the economy was healthier than it had been a few years earlier. But as Dave Marsh reasoned, if that was the case, "Why not platinum Ry Cooder?" Maybe it was true that the album's sales reflected the improvements to the music business' corporate infrastructure, but this reasoning does not fully account for the legend.

The real key to *Rumours's* place in public affection lies between the lines of the songs. Writing in *Trouser Press* in the early 1980s, Chris Salewicz pointed out that the album's theme of relationship torment resonated profoundly with listeners in their twenties and thirties. *Rumours* was the album that cemented the genre of album-oriented rock. Mickey Shapiro observes that the level of discussion was more complex and adult than the romantic angst usually found in pop music: "There was a real unabashed honesty in talking about relationships—not, 'Hey, baby you're cool, let's jump in the car and go to the hamburger stand.' The *Rumours* record was so explicitly personal, and the relationships were so in your face. 'Go Your Own Way'—not very subtle!

"Now, I don't want to say there's a relationship between the development of *Rumours* and cognitive therapy [laughs]. On the other hand, I do think there is some nexus to the way they [Fleetwood Mac and the Cognitive Therapy movement] approached subject matter. In those days there were the so-called underground heavy groups, who were playing guitar-driven, heavy, Jimmy Page stuff, and then you had pop groups who were kind of frothy. What I think was striking was the subject matter of their [Fleetwood Mac's] songs. They weren't hiding behind the facade of being rock musicians. They were talking about their own lives in very clear terms. 'Go Your Own Way'—there wasn't much ambiguity. On the flip side you have 'The Chain,' which seems to say [that] at the end of the day, friendships and mutual affection have a stronger force than romantic love or connectivity on a sexual basis. That record seemed to say that families survive despite the fact that they hate each other now and again."

Despite epitomizing the hedonistic, rock 'n' roll "L.A. cool" of the 1970s, Fleetwood Mac explored emotional gray areas of real life in their songs, and were a precursor to artists such as Phil Collins—a master of relationship ambivalence.

Says Shapiro, "In those days, there was a sex, drugs, and rock 'n' roll thing, the ethos of sexual promiscuity. Then you have the kind of sappy love songs. *Then* you had Fleetwood Mac saying, 'romance, love, relationships are very complex.' To have 'Go Your Own Way' and 'The Chain' on one record was an extraordinarily expansive emotionality, expressing the ambiguity we all sometimes feel in relationships. When there's a rough time there's a natural psychological desire to run away, *and* there's a natural desire to be connected to people who, at times, we are less than thrilled with. That's what families are all about when they have squabbles; blood is thicker than water."

Life's interpersonal relationships had been elevated to an art form, and the drama carried on offstage with a supporting cast of rock's glitterati. The Eagles' Don Henley had a starring role as the jet-set "love 'em and leave 'em suitor,"[9] who flamboyantly wooed Nicks in full view of the rest of the band, and who supposedly wrote "Life in the Fast Lane" about Buckingham and Nicks.

While *Rumours* made Number One in the United States two months after its release, it was a somewhat different story in the United Kingdom. Even though the album eventually hit Number One there as well, it was not a cultural phenomenon. Looking at the Top 40 singles chart of 1977, one would hardly know the album was out. The main television outlet for pop music was the BBC's weekly *Top of the Pops*, and its chart rundown was a truncated Top Thirty,

---

9 Refers to an actual Eagles in-joke, that sends up their usage of personal jets to shuttle the band members' dates back and forth to wherever they might be.

which gave the *Rumours* singles even less visibility. It was a similar story on the BBC's sole pop radio station, Radio 1.

It wasn't that the United Kingdom didn't want to buy American music; American R&B and dance music had always been a popular part of both the mainstream and underground music markets. The singles-buying public in Britain also had a great fondness for the maudlin side of country music—for instance, the impoverished and cuckolded farmer in Kenny Rogers's pity waltz, "Lucille," made a lot of friends in early 1977. There was also a fierce appetite for novelty records— the Muppets charted effortlessly, whereas Boston's classic FM superhit, "More Than a Feeling," barely scraped the Top 20 that year. American artists attempting to scale the British singles charts did so at their own peril. They were likely to land next to the likes of Liverpool Football Club ("We Can Do It") and Black Gorilla ("Gimme Dat Banana").

American album-oriented rock just didn't resonate with the British daytime radio audience. For some mysterious reason, even the Eagles could not get a Number One hit in the official (BBC) singles chart. "Hotel California," the single, peaked at Number Eight. Maybe it was the lifestyle: the music of the Eagles and (the new) Fleetwood Mac spoke of a land of sunshine and spacious roads, of open opportunity and things that worked. The United Kingdom of the 1970s was a land of buses and clouds, of restricted hours and musty resignation. Radio 1 rarely played rock and progressive music, with the exception of the *Johnny Walker Show*. Walker, however, had left the BBC before *Rumours* was released. In 1977, the Fleetwood Mac single most likely to be played on BBC radio would still be "Albatross."

But the album charts told a different story. It was here that progressive bands such as Genesis and Deep Purple made their stand. *Rumours* reached Number One in Britain in January 1978, after its singles had barely made a dent in the charts. How did people know it was out there? While progressive rock had always had its underground audience based around the student-union bars and venues, FM rock, which had even more adult appeal, was lucky enough to come of age at the same time that independent radio was finally made legal. The formats of many regional commercial radio stations picked up where the now-extinct pirate radio stations of the 1960s left off. Genres that had been largely rejected by the British Broadcasting Corporation—FM album-oriented rock, as well as more laid-back and jazzy R&B genres—now had a home. These new stations began broadcasting in 1973, and by 1977 they were flourishing. More good timing for Fleetwood Mac.

In April 1977, Fleetwood Mac flew in to play a handful of dates in major U.K. cities to support the release of *Rumours*, before heading to western Europe. The grueling *Rumours* tour schedule was now under way and Fleetwood Mac was encountering problems. Already 17 of their scheduled 20 U.S. dates had been cancelled after Stevie Nicks's battered vocal chords finally gave out. *Musician* magazine's Dan Forte recalled the band's first show of 1977, a benefit for the Jacques Cousteau Society at the Berkeley Community Theater. Halfway through the set, the audience became aware that Stevie Nicks was having such trouble singing that she would not be able to continue; Christine and Lindsey became the focus of the performance. Nicks's battle with her strained throat was to be a long struggle, and it would torment her throughout the band's platinum reign.

In the summer of 1977, Michael Freeman was the tour manager for Chicago popsters Pezband, who were fortunate enough to be the only support band for Fleetwood Mac when they played Binghamton, New York, on this tour. The show was intended as a dress rehearsal for the upcoming Madison Square Garden shows at the end of June and Freeman remembers Fleetwood Mac's mood that night: "The band seemed wildly enthused, but nervous at the same time about what they were about to be doing. I remember having to go out and introduce Pezband, and a thousand Bic lighters lit up and a huge roar came from the multitude, and you suddenly have this real sense that this wasn't your average gig."

Watching Fleetwood Mac that night, Freeman understood the unique band dynamic, the separation of individuals, and the whole that was so much greater than the sum of its parts. "There was very individual energy going on in those different parts of the stage. It made you want to go and look at the individuals, watch them. Together they were Fleetwood Mac—it wasn't just one person standing up there being supported by four other musicians."

An August 1977 *Rolling Stone* review from their first night at Madison Square Garden details Nicks's ongoing problems. The previous night's performance in Syracuse had been canceled due to her vocal strain, and even her physical demeanor seemed unstable. Reviewer Peter Herbst described "frantic roadies" trailing Nicks as she teetered unsteadily at the stage's edge. However, reports of the next night's performance, also at Madison Square Garden, suggest she had recovered considerably. Nicks has said that, whenever she could, she'd visit a vocal specialist prior to high-profile performances to receive a shot that would reduce swelling in the cords. But this was only a temporary solution. She was told that she ran the risk of blowing her vocal cords "right out" of her throat. Luckily, a Beverly Hills specialist eventually came to the rescue, prescribing singing lessons and a three-days-on, two-days-off routine. She was also advised to try speaking at a higher pitch.

The band toured North America throughout the summer months, moving on to tour Australia and Japan in November and December. Mick Fleetwood arranged for a camera crew to shoot some candid film of the band's travels. Some of this footage has seen the light of day in a bootleg video affectionately likened by Fleetwood to Bob Dylan's "Basement Tapes." It's a combination of live performances, endless hours of backstage meanderings, and press conferences, during which the band members move slowly, absorbed in small tasks, waiting for the chaos around them to subside.

Lindsey Buckingham told Joe Smith, when interviewed for Smith's book *Off the Record*, that the presence of women in bands tends to make life on the road less debauched than it otherwise might have been. Shown backstage in this footage, Fleetwood Mac certainly seem to be a very mild-mannered but fun-loving lot. They mostly appear to be battling fatigue, doing so with practical jokes and saucy banter. They mill around in large, white, clinical dressing rooms, sometimes drinking wine, sometimes trying to sleep. A highlight is a rare sighting of modest Mo Ostin, relaxed and smiling, joking with Nicks as she gives a crew member a long hug good-bye.

In the performances captured on this film, Buckingham's guitar-hand is as expressive as Stevie Nicks's scarf, pulling and flailing at strings. Seen here, during an abrasive version of "Over My Head," he plays a little disco and a little new wave. His bluesy twists are right on the money, as he rocks over his guitar in time to the riff, mop-top curls bouncing. It's a typical gig from the *Rumours* era: Christine is absorbed in her keyboard playing; she and John do not make much eye contact. John jams up front with the others, his playing fluid and effortless. Mick steps up front for his African talking drum solo in "World Turning," elbows churning, eyes popping.

The camera closes in as Stevie sings "Landslide," a black beret tipped aside a profusion of angelic Victorian curls, eyes fixed as if gazing at eternity itself. Throughout her early years with the band, up until the early 1980s, due to her extreme short-sightedness she was actually unable to see her audience. (She never wore her eyeglasses onstage; she once joked that her magical outlook on life arose from the fact that everytime she looked at a light, it turned into a star.) She sheds her wrap and reveals a gorgeous plunging halter with little spaghetti ties. Standing in front of a wind machine, she takes a chiffon-and-velvet scarf and strikes a pose, arching her torso. Her stage movements, she has said, came out of some "modern jazz and weird dancing" classes, and she's always been a fan of big gestures and bigger hand movements.

Nicks's frequent choice of all-black outfits was quite unusual, given the band's southern California pedigree. "The whole look was unusual!" laughs designer Margi Kent. "At points in her career she got ridiculed for [that look]—but later, Anna Sui, everybody copied it in their collections, so that's been complimentary for her. We did do clothes in all different colors, from the boots up, in tones of rusty, blood red, which was one of her favorites. We did hand-painted, dusty pastels; we did a very soft whisper pink—she really loved the pinky tones from the 1930s."

In many ways Stevie Nicks was rock's first real Goth girl. "Stevie is hard to categorize," says Kent. "No one else could really carry off what she does. Heart got into a drapey, flowy kind of thing for a tour, but it didn't work 'cause it wasn't them; they had their own identity. It's an integral part of Stevie and her performance; it frees her to do what she wants to do on stage. She is very physical with her clothes and her voice. [Her performance] had its own visual impact without the music, but you could tell what the music would sound like by her movements; it really translated beautifully."

Margi Kent also did clothes for others in the band. "I did a couple of tours for Mick and Lindsey, and did Christine for three tours. They were wonderful people. Stevie has a real strong image. Mick, too. It appeared then that Lindsey didn't want a [theatrical] image, he was wearing Armani suits and jackets, which were cool and he looked good—they weren't stage clothes, though. It was intense. His jackets would get drenched—totally wet, *really*, and he had to have several of them so they could dry out. It was really problematic, because they're in wardrobe cases and they can't air out properly. You're constantly trying to get them cleaned and dried, [using] hairdryers, fans, whatever's there; the wardrobers have their tricks. I think he stopped wearing jackets after that. You can do an Armani look and have it *not* be like that, but he's into his sound and not into what he looks like."

The one person for whom Kent didn't design was John McVie, the anti-image king known for his cut-off jeans and scruffy baseball caps. There is a segment in the *Rumours* bootleg video that perfectly captures John McVie's relationship with fashion. He is backstage in Japan, clad in a Malibu Beach style white shirt and pants, and he is checking himself in the mirror. He takes a few moments to gauge his midriff area, which he has exaggeratedly puffed out. He surveys the damage as he carefully pinches around his waist. Then, perfectly deadpan, McVie lights an elegant cigarette. Done!

This same video also offers instructive glimpses into the temperament of Richard Dashut. In a dressing room, he is explaining to Mick Fleetwood that there have been problems adjusting their sound system to the smaller halls they are playing in Japan, and that there have been no sound checks. No response from Fleetwood. Dashut ventures to restate the situation a little more bluntly; actually, there *are* sound checks; it's just that *no one* shows up to them. Still tactful, he attempts to make plans for a sound check the next day.

At this juncture, Mick Fleetwood leaves wordlessly. Obviously, the background to the encounter is unclear; Fleetwood isn't necessarily being uncooperative. Dashut, of course, true to form, stays patient and even throughout. The scene shifts to Buckingham who is sketching out a beautiful Elizabethan blues number on an acoustic guitar and talking to Dashut about the low end on a Beach Boys recording. The camera cuts to Dashut. He is listening, still with that even, Cheshire cat grin. The scene shifts again, this time to Stevie Nicks at a ballet bar, performing stretches prior to going on stage. She hails Dashut and insists he try the moves. He obliges, falls over, checks his groin, and limps off, still smiling the smile that must surely have been specified in his contract.

The film continues. The band has now played 98 gigs since February 1977. Lindsey is sick of playing; Christine's eyes are running. She and Mick have to wrap their wrists and fingertips in tape and bandages, in order to keep the split skin and worn tendons from getting the better of them. Stevie looks exhausted as she begins her makeup. Her unadorned face is drawn and thin, and her eyes are dark-circled. There are some long hypnotic minutes of Stevie doing her hair— teasing, spraying, pinning, combing. Stevie's friend, the late Robin Anderson, is helping her get dressed, and he prepares a device that emits gusts of steam. Nicks plunges face-first into it and stays in there for some time. Robin explains to the camera that it's a facial sauna, recommended by Boz Scaggs for breaking up congestion and warming up vocal cords.

It was around this time, according to both Mick Fleetwood and Stevie Nicks, that Nicks and Fleetwood embarked upon a sporadic two-year affair. It was not a public relationship at the time, a fact supported by the aforementioned video, where the two appear no more than friendly. Romantics will be pleased to know that, years later, Stevie Nicks told Courtney Love that Mick Fleetwood was, to her admitted surprise, one of her "great, great loves."

For his part, Fleetwood told Gavin Martin, in an interview in *The Sunday Express*, that theirs was a "magical mystery between two souls," albeit one that shouldn't have gone as far as it did. It is typical of Fleetwood's desire for harmony between all that he, Nicks, and his current wife still spend time together. Said Fleetwood, "It's how I was brought up."

This also speaks to the band's refusal to pretend that the difficult personal relationships never happened—a perpetual theme for all the band members, and something that was directly communicated to their audiences. One of Nicks's most endearing features is that she does not make excuses for her past, even when she might regret experiencing pain, or behaving in a way that hurt others; she embraces it all. The entire band have all been very candid about their personal shortcomings; they do not attempt to palm off their responsibilities on to anyone else, and it is this willingness to be human that has kept them—and *Rumours*—in the public's affections for decades.

I know I'm not wrong

Remarkably, in between shifting tons of vinyl and getting divorced, Fleetwood Mac found time to work with other artists. Mick Fleetwood especially went out of his way to extend a helping hand to those who had helped the band in the past, most notably Peter Green and Bob Welch.

Peter Green's story during the mid-1970s was a painful one. Christine McVie recalls him visiting them at a London hotel in mid-1976 during a brief U.K. tour. He was physically changed, and not in the best of health, either mentally or physically. Then there was the infamous incident with the shotgun and the accountant, in which Green took issue with the $30,000-per-year that the Fleetwood Mac back catalog was generating. Green was sentenced, at London's Marylebone Court, to a spell of psychiatric treatment. After being released, Green moved to the United States in 1977, and he was even married at Fleetwood's L.A. home.

By January 1978, the *New Musical Express*'s Steve Clarke found Mick Fleetwood taking care of a new and improved Peter Green, giving him the opportunity to relaunch his solo career. Of course, this didn't mean that Green would go for it in the way most artists would. His ambivalence about making money remained and he rejected a contract negotiated for him by Fleetwood. Says Bob Brunning, "I believe he did turn down a million-dollar contract. He was going through a very funny phase then about money."

Seedy Management obviously took a hit, both to its accounts and its morale, when Green refused to sign what he thought was a contract with Satan (ironically, it was actually a contract with the sainted Mo Ostin). Fleetwood told Steve Clarke, in the same interview, that although their company was a business, it was not primarily profit-driven. He noted that success made it hard to keep motivation pure. Now it was time to walk the talk; many people had invested their time and hopes in Green's new venture, but they had to accept his artistic and moral decision. The advance was returned to Warner Brothers.

Fleetwood also took a great interest in the solo career of Bob Welch, who had formed the rock trio Paris after quitting Fleetwood Mac. In November 1977 Welch released his album *French Kiss* and soon had a hit single on his hands, chosen by Fleetwood himself. It was the old Fleetwood Mac favorite, "Sentimental Lady." Fleetwood Mac and Bob Welch even went on tour together in mid-1978, during those golden years of mutual success when both *Rumours* and *French Kiss* were riding high. Welch had left Fleetwood Mac of his own volition, and the band was fond of him.

"I have a great deal of love for Bob Welch," said Christine at the time, and she's not a woman to throw her feelings around lightly. That they could now see him share good times after the rough years of the early 1970s was a source of great satisfaction. Luckily, none of the artists concerned had access to a rock 'n' roll crystal ball, which would have shown them the royalty dispute that would sour their relations fifteen or so years down the line. During the prime of *French Kiss*, Fleetwood auditioned band members for Welch's touring band and even offered him the use of their own road crew. Just before getting down to *Tusk*, Fleetwood Mac crammed in as much extracurricular activity as they could. Buckingham worked with New York singer-songwriter Walter Egan on his second album, *Not Shy*. He and Nicks had both worked on Egan's first album, and the two now helped out Lindsey's old pal Warren Zevon, who was recording his *Excitable Boy* album with the help of guitarist Waddy Wachtel.

This was the LP that contained Zevon's best-known single, "Werewolves of London." In June 1978, Wachtel and Zevon were auditioning rhythm sections for this song; they had gone through some of the best session players around, but they could not get the "animal" feel that they felt the song needed. Then somebody mentioned Mick Fleetwood and John McVie. They were just the ticket. Wachtel remembered the session with a laugh. The second take was deemed to be good, but not quite there. Fleetwood, wild-eyed and determined, insisted they keep going "to get it absolutely right." At 6:00 A.M., after around 60 takes, the producer decided that although Mick could take the pace, the rest of them couldn't. They listened to take two again and pronounced it a keeper. And it was—Fleetwood and McVie knocked the rhythm right into the pocket in one of the most distinctive accompaniments in pop history.

In March 1978 Fleetwood and Mickey Shapiro worked on an ambitious charity project that, if successful, would have made Fleetwood Mac one of the first western-style rock bands to play in the still-insular Soviet Union. The Russian authorities seemed receptive to the idea; evidently, their only question had been whether or not John McVie's cutoff jeans were actually his stage attire. The July dates were, sadly, canceled when the political situation in Afghanistan made the visit impracticable.

There's a famous incident, recounted by Fleetwood in his autobiography, of a three-day discussion which took place at Fleetwood's house during the early days of recording *Tusk*, the follow-up album to *Rumours*. This discussion involved Buckingham and the drummer and addressed the future of the *Tusk* project—and of the band itself. Buckingham was feeling creatively cramped within the band. He has admitted to feeling that Nicks had an easier time in the new band than he did. She did not take anyone's place. He, however, as the designated male vocalist and solo guitarist, had to keep playing Peter Green and Bob Welch songs. For Buckingham, an independent soul who tended to get lost for days in his own head when recording, this was a tough discipline.

Fleetwood, by now a master of these interpersonal band dilemmas, pointed out to Buckingham that he was either part of a band or he wasn't. Whether or not Buckingham was actually prepared to leave at this point is not a matter of public record. Fleetwood, ever the pragmatist, then asked Buckingham how he might be prepared to work on the next project and the answer was, more or less, "On my own." Fleetwood's attitude was, if it's good then go ahead. That Buckingham wanted to also have a hand in playing drums and bass, and that he wanted to do much of the creation in his home studio, did not concern Fleetwood. It is said that the McVies were not quite so thrilled.

Nonetheless, they all came together in the first months of 1978 to begin album rehearsals in a home rented in the

Hollywood Hills. During this time, John McVie entered his second marriage, this time to Julie Rubens, his 25-year-old secretary. It marked a new era for John, a time of domestic harmony, and this happiness greatly improved relations between Christine McVie and her new beau. The wedding ceremony was an intimate affair, and it was attended by band members, present and past, including Green, Welch, and the entire *Rumours* crew. John Mayall, McVie's former Bluesbreakers boss, flew over to join the celebrations. It was at this cordial event that Lindsey Buckingham joked to a *Rolling Stone* reporter that he hoped their audience would like the band in their new happy mode. It was a joke, and this was the music business.

They were already thinking of doing a double album to accommodate all the new songs that had accumulated among the band's three songwriters. The ever-present specter of creative frustration had to be exorcised. The record industry was in a dismaying slump and its gaudy godsend, disco, was on life support. The economy was faltering and people were sweeping away the 1970s in preparation for the new decade—not the best time for a bunch of privileged rock stars to release a double album of songs that bore little relation to each other and that were not guaranteed to appeal to the audience of millions who had bought their last album.

Buckingham was captivated by the sound of bands like the Clash and Talking Heads, and he wanted to inject the same energy and approach into Fleetwood Mac's music. He later explained how hard it was being the only one who felt this way, bemoaning the fact that Nicks played only the Doobie Brothers and Steve Miller in her dressing room. In fact, *Tusk*, heard from a distance, sounds like a young teenager on vacation with his folks, desperately signaling his otherness to anyone who might care. Ken Caillat, writing for *The Penguin*, recalls how Buckingham showed up at the studio on the first day with all of his hair cut off; the rest of the band exchanged glances and thought to themselves, "Uh-oh." Fleetwood was at first a little defensive, noting that the same musical snobs who were now calling him a dinosaur were the same kind of people who dismissed "Albatross" 10 years before. He was right. And so was Lindsey Buckingham.

The band was determined not to spend this album moving from studio to studio, so they installed themselves in Studio D at the Village Recorder in Los Angeles and built themselves a room there that exists to this day. The album cost them $1.4 million to record. Nicks told writer Phil Sutcliffe that they installed two ivory tusks "as tall as Mick" on either side of the console. The console became *Tusk* and the band became the tribe that worshipped the *Tusk* entity.

Fleetwood Mac invited a documentary crew into the studio and, later, on the road with them, to record the *Tusk* experience. The video, which was made commercially available, is a sedate affair. Watching it, one does not sense that this was an indulgent project. In it, Lindsey Buckingham muses on his role in the band, on how much of his being the studio takes. He says that he doesn't think his main contribution to the band is as a writer or guitar player, but as someone who is able to infuse other players with a new energy, and who knows how to arrange their work in the studio. This is certainly his special gift, but one can hardly overlook his musical contributions. The album is sequenced in such a way that the listener cannot get comfy with, say, a Christine song, because one of Lindsey's madcap, distorted stomps is up next. It can be disconcerting, and it is tempting to separate the artists, to get a better feel for their own personal evolution within the two discs.

Christine McVie's songs begin and end *Tusk*. Stevie Nicks may have been the most recognizable face of Fleetwood Mac, but she took a lot of critical teasing for her witchy ways and fog machines. It's quiet Christine who is the keeper of the flame. "Over And Over" leads us gently—maybe too gently—into *Tusk*. It has a lovely, intimate vocal sound, hazy and gentle, with warm slide guitars and distant floating choirs of Nicks. Already the harmonies are more ethereal than the Brian Wilson-layered chorales on *Rumours*. The drums are clickier and the bass is understated; it's a much more casual approach, and some of it might be lost on a car radio. McVie's "Think About Me" is a little more familiar, another of her bounding, ker-plunk-a-plunk blues tunes. For fans of the bass-and-drum vibe of *Rumours*, this Grateful Deadish boogie is a little toppy, but it's a great pop song.

So far, it seems that all Buckingham did was thin out the sound of the instruments compared to the fuller bodied sound of *Rumours*. However, this does compel the listener to focus on the beautifully landscaped vocal melodies of Christine's "Brown Eyes" and "Honey Hi." "Brown Eyes" is a gloriously meditative jazz-pop piece, and has an interesting continuity with the track it follows, Buckingham's "That's Enough for Me." Again, the vocal timbres of Lindsey and Christine are curiously similar, which is always a perverse delight. "Brown Eyes" is a very spacious, utterly addictive mood piece. It's less structured than most of Christine's songs, and it makes a great companion to "That's All for Everyone." A gorgeous, floaty sha-la-la chorus and unresolved dabblings of keys and strings make this one of the album's best tracks.

Of course, it has to compete with one of her best songs, the bravely sweet "Never Make Me Cry." The melody and treatment are conventional Christine, but there's something extra-special about the vocal. It's not quite note perfect, but her tone and phrasing are tender and vulnerable, and the accompaniment sounds sympathetically faded.

"Honey Hi" is a slighter Christine song with some magical harmonies. One can hear how this might have been given a setting of more traditional, rhythmic McVie-isms. Instead, the arrangements are bolstered by deep waves of vocal harmonies and tasteful counterpoint. The collection ends, rather informally, with her "Never Forget." This is a very mid-to-late-1970s song, with a pleasing, airy melody line and an easy nature: it could have been an upbeat England Dan & John Ford Coley number. It was a popular track with reviewers at the time of *Tusk*'s release.

Tusk is not Stevie Nicks's best showing (yes, there are legions who would argue to the contrary, brandishing "Sara" and "Beautiful Child" as life-changing songs). Nicks wrote some wonderful songs, which were well treated, but her later pieces seem to need their own space in which to languish. By the time *Tusk* was recorded, her voice had acquired some new dimensions—it sounds chestier, raspier, and looser—but the world would have to wait for her first solo album to hear her at her best. That is not to say she held back; she threw herself into each song with determination.

"Sara,"[10] a song that was the subject of a copyright lawsuit that Nicks ultimately won, sounds rather like "Dreams" with no makeup. Like Christine's first two songs, it seems to be missing the Fleetwood Mac's golden bottom; the rhythm section again seems to be lacking in presence. Again, this deliberate dressing down of the song's presence prepares the listener well for Nicks's gorgeous, swirling rainy-day marathon, "Storms." Nicks is one of Nashville's great, lost artists; she could have been out there with Tammy, Dolly, and Loretta. Maybe if her father had not taken her to live in San Francisco, it would have been a different story.

"Sisters of the Moon" is one of Nicks's most celebrated mystical epics, and it seems to beg to be followed by more songs in this vein. There is some fabulous Heart-like guitar squealing from Buckingham, and Nicks's vocal vamping is bluesy and raw. One reviewer, Stephen Holden, likened her to a West Coast Patti Smith. Indeed, the song does sound like a visceral rock jam from 1975. The chorus is classic Fleetwood Mac, and is driven by Christine's jaunty Clavinet.

"Angel," the compelling, tiny foot stomper that opens side three, would have been a great *Rumours II* track. Nicks, said Buckingham, writes her songs as simple loops, around which she weaves a melodic thread. You can hear what he means in this song. The verses and choruses blend easily into each other, and Buckingham's arrangements keep things seamless

---

[10] This song appeared on the original CD release of *Tusk* in an edited form, much to the distress of the fans. Echoing the saga of "Silver Springs," it was cut down in order to fit the whole double album on a single disc. Also meddled with was Buckingham's "I Know I'm Not Wrong" which was remixed for the CD release.

without being bland. The *Tusk* video shows Nicks working with Buckingham, dissecting the gutsy harmony in the chorus. These moments of vocal splendor don't happen by accident.

Certainly, "Beautiful Child" didn't. Nicks's last song on the album is a rich and captivating ballad, slightly mournful and rather Kate Bush-like in its plaintive nature. Once more, the counterpoint vocal parts, which here carry a more complex melody than the lead, give the song enchanting depth, and the song appears to reflect from different angles with each new playing.

And so, to Mr. B. When *Tusk* was recorded, this new fan of punk rock had a lot to prove when it came to street cred. First of all, he came from California and thus, without ever really trying, was one of the Beautiful People. He had spent thousands of dollars and countless months recording carefully structured albums and was rewarded with millions of dollars. Worst of all, his music made people happy. It was easy on the ear and well played. He was a rich musician who at times could have passed for a hippie, and people liked him. What could he possibly have to say that was new?

Admittedly, "The Ledge"—Buckingham's "Janie Jones"— was nothing new, but it was certainly a new configuration of familiar sounds and techniques. Here, the munchkins invade CBGB's, a wacky vocal sits atop a silly, rigid, new wave back-beat. A fabulous simple guitar solo bridges the song. Buckingham's playing, seen through the late 1970s prism of punk-rock primitivism, may have sounded a little too fluid and well done. But in retrospect, it is absolutely perfect.

There's a scene on the *Tusk* video in which Buckingham is singing "Save Me a Place" in Studio D at the Village

Recorder. Dashut is in the control room with Mick Fleetwood, who is wearing a "very L.A." white suit and scarf. Buckingham asks Mick Fleetwood how he'd feel about doing a drum track. They confer with producer Richard Dashut. Buckingham and Dashut animatedly discuss possibilities. Fleetwood, storklike, appears to be considering something: will he play drums, or morph into John Cleese and do a silly walk? The drum sound of the song grabs the listener's attention because it is so boxy and willfully lo-fi. Its purpose is to complement the vocal harmonies, a 21st-century alt country blend that is all heart and no gloss. Sublime.

In an interview with *Modern Drummer*, Mick Fleetwood noted that Buckingham seemed wary of asking the others to participate in some of his more unusual sound-making experiments. Fleetwood, on the contrary, was not only open to this adventure, but had had prior experience of working with nonconventional percussion. In the Jeremy Spencer days of the old Fleetwood Mac, they had close-mic'd a pencil hitting a chair to get a particular rhythmic texture. What's more, Fleetwood had been present at the recording of the Beatles' "Maxwell's Silver Hammer," and was much impressed when they brought a real anvil into the studio. At one time Fleetwood sought to have the sound of his leg being slapped as a rhythmic patch; when he found the real thing wasn't leggy enough, they sent for a leg of lamb from a butcher and used that instead.

These experiences were drawn upon when perfecting the "drum" sound on "What Makes You Think You're the One." In order to get a "suck and push" sound, the band used the sound of Buckingham's tape player recorded on open mics, with the overloaded signal going straight to tape. This sets the tone for the song; "What Makes You Think You're the One" is not at all sublime. It's a mad catharsis of crashing drums that certainly has its place in the universe, but is just a little too jolting in the context of this album.

Buckingham finally loses his self-consciousness in "That's All for Everyone." It is a psychedelic masterpiece, a song that sounds like it fell off the Beatles' *White Album* and perhaps collided with the United States of America's "Garden of Earthly Delights." This song's beauty cannot be understated. It is less a linear melody than a series of textures, of small sweet phrases, a ravishing split from the space-time continuum. Then it's back to the herky-jerky new wave thing; the bonkers "Not That Funny" comes from the land of Devo. As with Devo, the crafty musicianship speaks of skillful players slumming it, but a driving simple groove and a great buzzsaw bass rescue the song from condescension.

Finally, Buckingham comes up with a piece that brings together all the wildly disparate elements on *Tusk*. With "That's Enough for Me," one just has to stand back and take a deep breath. This one comes charging out of the gate with the full force of the writer's creativity. It has a complicated rhythm, a two-step, madcap polka with an entire other song layered over the top, and is rendered in a bizarre, androgynous whine—another completely captivating vocal sound from Caillat and the crew. The star of the song is a world-class, breakneck, bluegrass, finger-perfect guitar solo.

Several members of the band have quoted an apocryphal story that tells how, when the people at Warner Brothers heard the album *Tusk*, they saw their Christmas bonuses flying out of the window. By the time they got to this track, they probably saw those bonuses running to the edge of the Pacific shore, stripping off their clothes, and wading deep into the blue. Those bonuses were *gone*—but that guitar part is just amazing.

The mad two-stepping band from "The Ledge" returns for "I Know I'm Not Wrong." A silly little synth riff toward the end puts an odd-sounding date stamp on the piece and is, in its perky way, the most jarring element on the album. This song is another piece of brilliant concision, with a half-stated simple three-note chorus. The not-quite-there quality that Buckingham manages to coax out of his higher vocal register is also present in "Walk A Thin Line," making the chorus of that song equally addictive. There are some very familiar-sounding melodic hints in here; some of them might even have once belonged to John Lennon or the Beach Boys, but they are so refreshingly recycled.

"Walk a Thin Line" is another great instance of secondary vocal parts being used to define the song, so that the lead vocal is cut free and the song appears to float. As usual, Buckingham plays most of the instruments, including the harmonica. Assistant engineer on *Tusk*, Hernan Rojas, a Chilean musician and producer, recalled on *The Penguin* that many of the drum tracks on the album were doubled and tripled; they were in search of the "Phil Spector Wall of Sound" quality. It is an album, said Rojas, that benefits from being heard over headphones, a process that, in true Brian Wilson and Beatles tradition, yields hidden treasures.

Buckingham's "Tusk" is the second-to-last song on the album and is one of the oddest Fleetwood Mac tracks of all time. It begins with a crazed little Balkan beat underneath a sinister half-hidden vocal. Then the chorus suddenly snaps out of the speakers like angry housecats on the attack. It is the sound of Fleetwood Mac shrieking at each other: "Don't say that you love me." "Tusk" has since become best known for the guest appearance by the University of Southern California's Trojan Marching Band, a musical adventure of Fleetwood's devising.[11]

In an interview with Tom Lanham in *Guitar One* magazine, Buckingham commented on the different writing process of this album. *Rumours* was a group effort; ideas were shared and verbalized, and players were directed. It was, Buckingham said, like making a movie. *Tusk*, however, was more like making a painting. He was able to work in the way he had while in Buckingham Nicks, going straight from his home-taped sketches to the recording studio, working alone.

This new, more insular approach did not go down well with John McVie, who had spent 10 years with Fleetwood Mac, doing it the old way, trying out the songs together. His ambivalence was symbolized by his absence from the video for the single "Tusk," where he was represented by a life-sized cutout of himself. In turn, Buckingham's sense of isolation is vividly reflected in his songs, tempered as they are by a grim sense of humor.

This isolation is sadly examined in "Save Me a Place," in which he laments the demon within that drives him into self-exile; the singular loneliness of the loner. As the album progresses, his disillusion becomes clear, as does his

---

[11] See Chapter 12.

desperation ("That's All for Everyone"); everything has soured ("Not That Funny") and, worse still, it would appear that he is alone with his vision: "But no one was listening, I walk a thin line" ("I Walk a Thin Line").

The listener gets the impression that the man is barely hanging on, and it was true. Even while, in the eyes of many, he was indulging himself in the making of *Tusk*, Buckingham did have to live in the knowledge that he ploughed a solitary furrow. In *Tusk*, the recriminations of the *Rumours* songs have turned to something more sad and desperate.

It was during the recording of *Tusk* that Christine met her new love, Dennis Wilson, the Beach Boys' drummer and resident bad boy. It was, she has said, a very intense time, and this romantic uncertainty is the underlying theme of all her songs on *Tusk*. The saddest part of her songs is her acceptance of this lack of emotional security. For example, the sad Christine of "Never Make Me Cry," is happy to have the love of her beloved, even if it isn't undivided.

It is not new territory for Christine, but it is unusual that all her contributions are built around this bittersweet core, even when the musical setting belies the sentiment, as in the bouncy "Think About Me," where McVie accepts that it's her willingness to give her honey a free rein that keeps her in his affections.

The songs of Stevie Nicks reflect themes similar to those of Lindsey Buckingham, albeit from a more windswept and raven-studded perspective. As Ken Caillat commented in *The Penguin*, Nicks is far more at ease with other people than Buckingham, and this is reflected in the absence of alienation in her songs. For Nicks, it appears that the pain of the

Rumours years has not faded; it has simply been afforded a new perspective. Her epic "Sara" seems to focus on a troubled other, rather than on herself; here there are two restless souls, the other more of a wanderer than Nicks herself.

Although her songs are not the succinct folk-pop offerings found on *Rumours*—they sometimes ramble—her lyrics are stronger. Her Brontë Goth sensibilities are given free rein in "Storms" and "Sisters Of The Moon." She speaks of something long lost, and still, there is the Cathy and Heathcliffe saga, continued in "Angel," where the two lovers pretend there has been an end, knowing that there could never be anything of the sort.

None of her songs suggest there has been any closure; on the contrary, the saga is definitely to be continued. Indeed, in later years, Mick Fleetwood identified *Tusk*—an ensemble solo album—as the reason the band was able to stay together in the years after *Rumours*. In *Tusk*, the individuality of each writer is allowed to grow, and in this apparent separation, the band members are given the space they needed to redefine themselves before coming together again.

tusk!

Rumours was the right record at the right time, there is no disputing that. Although *Tusk* may not have been the *wrong* record, it was certainly released at the wrong time. "The market crashed at retail in 1979," says Mickey Shapiro. "People stopped listening to radio, and records weren't really selling when *Tusk* came out—and *Tusk* was supposed to be their savior—I hate to use that term." It was no secret that Warner Brothers was hoping for a *Rumours II* to turn their luck around. Mickey Shapiro remembers the record company reaction was much more sympathetic.

"Mo Ostin walked into my office, and they were all sitting there, and he said, 'Listen, I respect you guys.' And at this time, at the height of their success, they did have this feeling of omnipotence. I'm not saying that was egos gone amok: they *had* accomplished something. Mo Ostin said, 'Listen, boys and girls'—and he was actually very sweet—'I'm here to tell you something. You can do what you want, but we've done our research, and I can tell you, retail's on its ass; records aren't selling and we think a double album is a really bad idea. Not that [*Tusk*] isn't good on a qualitative basis, but we think the market will have a very difficult time absorbing it. Do as you will!' And he left the room.

"The band said, 'We're going to go with it.' I called him up and he said, 'Hey, I respect that.' He was extraordinarily deferential, and I think, retrospectively, was giving them very good advice [at the time]. I have to say I have great respect for that man. It was nothing like, 'Here's a lecture.' It was, 'I want to share these thoughts.' At that time [Fleetwood Mac] were feeling pretty powerful—that they knew more than anybody else knew—and I don't mean that in a cynical way. It was done in a very nice ... I don't want to imply there was any acrimony. He came to the office and everyone had a coffee and he said, 'Listen, I want to share this with you.' [The band] thought that they would transcend it."

And, as Shapiro states, the label did support the band. The November 1, 1979 issue of *Rolling Stone* reported that Warner Brothers was unveiling its largest-ever promotional campaign; its object—*Tusk*. The campaign would begin on October 17, 1979. They had, for the first time in their history, gone to an outside agency to promote the album, but the band eventually requested that Warner Brothers take the project in-house after all. The company's director of advertising, Shelley Cooper, said they "owed it to the band to exhaust every conceivable outlet," again a measure of good faith at the record company level.

The band rejected this campaign because they didn't want to be sold like chewing gum. Nonetheless, the *Tusk* campaign ended up being much more elaborate than the *Rumours* strategy. Its excesses reflected those indulged in during the recording of *Tusk*. A key graphic in the campaign was the famous anonymous dog (pictured attacking an anonymous human ankle) from the album artwork. Selected stores were also graced with a motorized floor display featuring a silk-screened image of the same dog. The budget, said Bob Regehr, was "huge" (he wouldn't go into specific numbers) and the expenditure would continue for "a long time to come."

"Tusk" was the first single from the album. It was Fleetwood's idea to release it, and again his wishes and his authority were respected by the label. Regehr told *Rolling Stone* that the song's release was intended as a "conversation piece. Something that would provoke people." Writer Phil Sutcliffe has likened its release to a "bizarre public health warning to *Rumours* purchasers." Provoke people it did.

The legend of "Tusk" has been bolstered by the legend of the guests on the track, the Trojan Marching Band from the University of Southern California. It was Fleetwood's idea to tour and have local brass bands guest wherever they played. That didn't happen, but this recording, and the video that went with it, served to cement the legend of the band's eccentricity and extravagance by using that most American and upbeat of all things, the college marching band.

Since he had the idea, Fleetwood paid for the proceedings. The band usually rehearsed on campus, but Fleetwood chose to rent Dodger Stadium for the day, and a smaller version of the marching band was rehearsed. Although Fleetwood has taken a lot of ridicule over the years for this extravagance, he has been rewarded over time. Fleetwood's idea is now deeply interwoven into collegiate culture: "Tusk" is now a staple of every college marching band's repertoire.

The USC Trojan Marching Band, with its famous colors of cardinal and gold, is probably the most visible marching band in the business. It has appeared in Super Bowl festivities and Oscar presentations, as well as on countless recordings, although "Tusk" is probably their most celebrated public appearance. The band has been under the leadership of its director Dr. Art Bartner and assistant director, Tony Fox, since the early 1970s. Under their guidance, the Trojan Marching Band became one of the first marching bands to incorporate contemporary rock and R&B in a repertoire that was usually dominated by military and classical standards.

Trojan Marching Band and "Tusk" alumnus Mark Myers takes a moment to approximate the sound heard by a typical band member in the middle of a full stadium. By all accounts, it's an overwhelming experience. The phone line echoes with his imitation, the sound of blasting white noise. The feeling, says Myers, is an incredible rush. Some people, he notes humorously, see football games as sporting events with some sort of half-time show, where one takes a break to buy beer. Bandies, on the other hand, see a half-time show with some sort of game on either side.

Being a Trojan is not for the faint of spirit. Gretchen Heffler was a trumpet player with the band when it performed on the "Tusk" recording. She recalls the rigors of band camp: "You're marching from nine 'til noon, and then again from two 'til five—and then there's evening rehearsal. You're marching all day in the sunshine, learning how to play, and marching in that high-stepping style—which is not easy to do, because your mouthpiece is bouncing all over your face."

Heffler remembers that Fleetwood found the band via John McVie, who had been a guest at a wedding where the band had played. Because the recording took place out of season, in June 1979, the band was smaller, at 112 members, than their usual complement of 230 members. Fleetwood went down to a band meeting to put across the "Tusk" idea to the Trojans. Heffler was at the meeting. "If you look at the "Tusk" video, where Mick stamps his foot and he bobs up and down and waves his hands, that's exactly what he showed us. The music was so out of the ordinary, out of their genre, when we heard it we all kind of went, 'whoa?'"

One of the Trojan band's signature qualities is a solid low end, which is much in keeping with the Fleetwood Mac philosophy. Heffler recalls, "Tony Fox worked on the charts, he's a great marching band arranger. He'll give strong voices to the bass, which gives a really good blend. If all you can hear are piccolos, you're going to have a headache! We got the written music and tried to play it. We were having issues with the rhythm and were getting frustrated—and so was the director. So we got a tape of Mick playing the drums; everyone in the band went, 'Ohhhhhh. So *that's* how it goes.'"

The "Tusk" video has a shot of Nicks, as Trojan for a day, marching and twirling a baton. Heffler remembers that the marching band's baton twirler had left her batons on the ground, and Nicks picked them up. "She said, 'I used to be a baton twirler in high school,' and she started to twirl. The rest of the band didn't really do anything like that."

It was a long day for the Spirit of Troy. Says Heffler, "We all went to the college bar and had martinis before the gig—oh yes, you've *got* to get up for the gig! I think we got to Dodger Stadium around 10:45, [and] we signed off on some waiver where we got paid one dollar. We all agreed to it—if you didn't want to be there, you could just not be there. [Fleetwood Mac] were waiting for us; they came to greet us with cases and cases of Heineken beer and food." The track was played back to the band over the stadium loudspeakers. "We played and recorded the song, then once we'd got it in the can, that's when we marched into the stadium in full uniform and they filmed that."

Not only did the Trojans reprise the song for *The Dance* in 1997, but they also still play it at least once every single game. They were awarded a platinum record for their efforts, and one year after "Tusk'"s release, Buckingham, Nicks, and Fleetwood joined the marching band at their halftime show. Nicks twirled, Fleetwood played the bass drum, and Buckingham conducted the band from the top of a 15-foot ladder.

Gretchen Heffler's reaction to the album when it was released echoed that of many people at the time. "I thought, 'we've just played on an album that's going to be a big flop.' We were known for playing on busting things; I mean, we were in *The Gong Show Movie*! But I recently purchased the album again, to have it on CD, and there's some *really* good stuff on there that I kind of discounted back then."

Tusk emerged within a complex array of cardboard sleeves with rather progressive-looking art and photo collages. It was dedicated to the memory of the recently deceased fathers of both Mick Fleetwood and Lindsey Buckingham. It sold for $15.98—quite a lot for its time—and, according to Fleetwood, many people chose to tape the album when the Westwood One radio corporation kindly broadcast it, uninterrupted, on the eve of its release.

Nonetheless, despite the reported dismay of those who hoped to share in its profits, *Tusk* went double platinum in 1984 (which, since it is a double album, is actually quadruple platinum)—hardly a disaster. Of course, it could have been a more profitable couple of years for the band. Many have questioned the decision to spend $1.4 million building onto someone else's studio. Says Bob Brunning, "Mick didn't always have his own way, but in certain areas he does have a lot of common sense, and he [soon realized] they could have bought a studio for themselves for the money they were spending on hire, and he was absolutely right."

That said, with the grueling years of nonstop touring, the success, the excess, and the need to get on and create, it would have been difficult to keep a sensible perspective. That they all made another album together is really the big story, for ever since the success of *Fleetwood Mac*, the band had been plagued with constant quizzing about exactly when they were splitting up. Stevie Nicks was happy to go on record about how much she disliked the packaging of *Tusk*, and that, although she loved the spirit of the album, she was not about to repeat the experience. Mick Fleetwood experienced similar ambivalence when the album was released, although he has insisted that *Tusk*, in retrospect, is his all-time favorite album.

And as for the music press: Mitch Cohen, writing for *Creem*, didn't like it. He especially didn't like Buckingham's contributions, and was undecided about Nicks's. He wrote an unforgettable description of her melodies, claiming they reminded him of "fruit suspended in Jell-O"—he must have been listening to "Beautiful Child." Christine he liked for her warmth and vulnerability. Cohen pinpointed *Tusk* as a "blissed-out image risk, though not a commercial one," rather late 1960s in its anti-ness. The album's length, he commented, makes it clear that Fleetwood Mac is really three bands.

It's an analysis echoed by many reviewers. *Rolling Stone's* Stephen Holden called *Tusk* "a mosaic of pop-rock fragments," and thought that it "ushers out the 1970s with a long melancholy sigh." He liked the album for what it tries to do, for the changes in pace that hold the two discs together, and for the use of background vocals as a substitute for strings and keyboard parts. "Brown Eyes," he surmises, "sounds like it was invented for the production rather than vice versa." Most critics received the album well and appreciated its complexities. Greil Marcus called it "subversive MOR, a change to the System from within."

When the album did not outsell *Rumours*, there was a backlash against Buckingham. *Tusk* was not an album one could look to and reach objective conclusions—one needed the passage of time for some perspective. Comments Ben Fong-Torres, "I'm not a believer that you are even a relative failure or that it was a mistake, when you reach that stellar level [of *Rumours*] and you don't match it. If that were the case then people like Michael Jackson and Madonna would just have to retire! If you're an artist you can't respond to the larger marketplace or to whatever anybody else is doing. That has certainly happened, but I don't think that Fleetwood Mac did." Fong-Torres concludes that all genres have their own following, and that an artist should rest easy in that knowledge. Otherwise, he says, "It's like being a football player wondering how the baseball player's going to affect your team."

There is no "despite" about *Tusk's* artistic appeal. There are admittedly a couple of songs that might have benefited from a more straightforward treatment, from being prettied up and bulked up so they sounded more like songs on the previous album—"Over and Over" and "Sara" come to mind—but there is far more to be gained from the destructuring of

Christine McVie's "Brown Eyes" and "Honey Hi." It is a very sophisticated album. *Rumours's* engineer, Ken Caillat, has said that he was vexed on occasion by Buckingham's willful contrariness, turning everything upside down and inverting his carefully set levels. "We were in strange territory," he noted on *The Penguin*, before adding that in retrospect, *Tusk*, with its bold risk taking, is his favorite Fleetwood Mac album.

But despite the anarchic attack on Caillat's console, there is nothing ham-fisted about the album. The vocals, for instance, are beautifully registered and blended, with an expansive spectrum of texture and timbre. A great deal of thought and attention went into them, it's clear. One of the charms of the album is what's not there, the stuff that is hinted at, in the foggy vagaries of "Walk a Thin Line" and "That's Enough for Me."

Caillat did not walk away from the album empty-handed; during its recording, he met the Village Recorder's lovely receptionist, Diane. He successfully elbowed away his rival for her hand—Richard Dashut—and the two had their first date at Dodger Stadium for the recording of "Tusk."

On October 12, 1979, *Tusk* was released and the band took to the road in November for what was to be a 13-month tour. They began the tour in Japan and Australia, then returned to the States for the summer. Then it was off to Europe and then back to America, finishing the tour in February 1980. The experience almost finished off the band—even the resilient Richard Dashut succumbed to road trauma. Nicks has recalled that the tour took every bit of inner strength—and there wasn't that much inner strength left after the *Rumours* ordeal.

The band was determined not to be miserable on this tour, and few expenses were spared. Hotel rooms were repainted for overnight stays; baby-grand pianos winched through hotel window frames; helicopters hovered at their beck and call. They made sure they were rarely reminded of the old days, of riding the interstates with everyone shoe-horned into a station wagon full of pot smoke and flight cases. A few years later, the band would cite this excess as an instance of Mick Fleetwood losing control of the band's spending. There would be bitter exchanges.

Fleetwood later commented in *Mojo* magazine that he and Courage had initially booked the band into cheaper hotels, but that the others had complained. The band's limo habit began to rival their supposed cocaine patronage; not only did each band member get a limousine, but the band's support staff were also given individual vehicles, taking their average number of limousines in use to 14 instead of five. Writer Phil Sutcliffe noted that John McVie decided to save himself some cash by traveling on the crew bus. This was McVie in so many ways; the practical-minded working musician who took so long to leave Bluesbreakers for the romance of life with Peter Green's band. McVie, the un-superstar, was the man least likely to suffer inflation of self-esteem.

The *Tusk* documentary captures the shows at the St. Louis, Missouri, Checkerdome on November 5 and 6, 1979. It's a very different-looking Lindsey Buckingham to the one that toured *Rumours*. Gone is the beard and bouncy curls. Instead, he has cropped hair, sculpted new wave cheekbones, and a suggestion of rather glam eye makeup. Buckingham's transformation alone dragged the band into the 1980s.

The band's dramatic power is greater than ever, and is, as usual, most in evidence during "The Chain." John McVie kicks into the chorus with massive authority, the notes landing like the steps of a terrible giant tromping across Lilliput. Nicks crouches low to the stage, like a desperate child, bashing her tambourine against the boards. On guitar, Buckingham flails his arms in the tradition of Pete Townshend. As usual, no matter how grueling the offstage schedule, when they are onstage, the band seem to be having the time of their lives.

The great irony is that, although *Tusk* was profoundly influenced by new wave, the cost was still that of an old school rock star. But one has to look beyond that. Really, the money meant nothing if that's what it took to hold the band together; it may have been the difference between *Tusk* and no album at all. Fleetwood is proud of the album, he has pointed out that spending over a million dollars on their craft was no sin. They were spending their own money, which they had earned the same way—by recording and touring.

Twenty odd years later, the world would come to agree with him, and with Buckingham. *Tusk* is now seen as one of rock's noble ventures, not only as a fine, imaginatively rendered collection of songs but also as an artistic statement of self-determination, a musician's refusal to be a people pleaser. It has attitude and substance, and in a way, it was the ultimate punk rock statement.

It was easy for the Clash to tear down the establishment; they were pulling someone else's house down. They had nothing to lose and everything to gain. Fleetwood Mac was the establishment, and people liked it that way. The band themselves had comfortable lifestyles and weren't ready to return to their day jobs. Now, that was admittedly unlikely, but don't forget, only one of them had acquired a college degree—and that was in sculpture. The band could have made a much cheaper statement and kept the cash, and then made their *real* follow-up. Buckingham had to live with the recriminations of others for two decades before the world caught up with him and *Tusk* became cited as a creative touchstone for the new musical highwaymen.

solos and so longs

At 10:50 P.M. on December 8, 1980, Mark Chapman, loitering outside the Dakota apartment building in the shade of Central Park, did what punk rock and even the ungainly death of Elvis had failed to do. He brought down the curtain on rock's first act with the four bullets that killed John Lennon. The Number One single at the time was Kenny Rogers's "Lady." Stevie Nicks was at home, finishing off a song written for her dying Uncle Jonathan. The song was titled "For John," and she happened to finish it that evening, before reports of the shooting made the news.

Fleetwood Mac's grueling *Tusk* tour was finally through. *Tusk* turned out to be the punctuation point between their shared history and their solo selves. Nicks told the press that, after *Tusk*, they were never going to do another Lindsey record on Fleetwood Mac time again. That was in 1980, and it's probably just as well not to read too much into it. The growing pains of the five people stepping out of their 1970s glory and into the eighties were apparent. These days, 20-plus years later, all the second guessings and what-were-we-thinkings are long flown, and the artistic statement made by the notorious double album can be seen in its proper perspective: as a statement of autonomy and integrity.

September 1980: The band divorced Mick Fleetwood by firing him as the band's manager. By the end of the *Tusk* tour, Nicks had finally hired hard-hitting Irving Azoff to take care of her career. The extravagances of the previous year on the road had eaten into profits. The press was in constant pursuit of the band, convinced they were going to split up at any second. Nerves were frayed and patience was tried. In a meeting that month, to which the other members had brought along their personal representatives, it was agreed that Seedy Management—which had come to mean Mick Fleetwood—was no longer in charge of the band's finances or career strategy.

It was clearly a blow for Fleetwood—as much to the heart as to the bank account. He noted in his memoirs that he had taken only 10 percent of the band's net earnings; it was customary for management to take their cut from gross earnings, and, for a band whose overheads were as high as Fleetwood Mac's, this was a huge difference in potential income. Says Bob Brunning, "Mick would be the first to argue that he's the worst manager of his own finances; it's all in his book. But I'd separate [that from] the leadership skills. And the other immense talent [apart from music] that he and John both had was spotting talent. My God, they could see it a mile off. Everytime the band faced disaster, they could pull them up, 'cause they could spot someone. Their instincts— they just know when it's right."

Not having any publishing income flow, Mick Fleetwood and John McVie were more dependent on working, both live and in the studio. Obviously, they needed an income stream, but it had always been about more than just the money. They still loved to play. Throughout his career with Fleetwood Mac, whether in good times or bad, Fleetwood had played constantly with friends, old and new. John McVie did so as well, but to a lesser degree, for he was often quoted as being happy to play his bass parts in the studio, and then leave to sail the oceans in his boat.

"John used to insist—once the songs were sorted—that he and Mick get the rhythm track down first, which of course is common practice. Getting all his parts finished and then leaving, he'd say, 'I can't stand all that sitting around, mixing,'" laughs Bob Brunning. "He'd do his bit in the studio and then go sailing. The band would be there another six months; he'd come back, and they'd give him the record. He thought that what was added on top was other people's business. They trusted Lindsey, and still do."

In 1980 Mick Fleetwood had finally persuaded his fellows to put together a live album, which the record company was also eager for, although it came several years after the live-release frenzy stoked by *Frampton Comes Alive!* The two-LP collection was assembled from the *Tusk* tour, with three new soundstage recordings added to leaven the oldies. Released at the end of 1980, it didn't sell as well as the industry had hoped, which was probably a matter of timing, the dwindling economy and the cultural changeover. The band would make a successful musical transition into the 1980s, but not enough time had passed at that point for them to be able to reintroduce their old 1970s selves.

And so, inevitably, it came to distances. The band began the decade by taking time out for themselves. Fleetwood really didn't want to, but recognized he didn't have a choice. He undertook a venture that would have made his dad, Wing Commander Fleetwood, proud. He repaired to Ghana with the ever-faithful Richard Dashut, who had presumably recovered from the *Tusk* ordeal. He also took a couple of recording consoles (one was sure to break, reasoned Fleetwood—and one did), plus musicians George Hawkins and Todd Sharp. Fleetwood noted in his auto-biography that he asked Bob Welch if he was up for the trip, but Welch declined. The resulting album was financed under a three-record deal with RCA. Warners' Mo Ostin had declined the project, which was to eventually cost half a million dollars. *The Visitor* was as notable for what it left behind in Africa as for what it brought back. This is not to say it is a slight album—there is a lot to like.

Fleetwood, in true Mick style, salted the local economy by hiring local drummers and choirs to accompany the western band on some straightforward versions of old Fleetwood Mac favorites such as "Rattlesnake Shake" and some *Visitor* band originals. There is little crossover in the manner of Paul Simon's *Graceland*, which appeared five years later; the Ghanaian musicians are given space for their own sharply separate songs. On most of these, Fleetwood, Hawkins, and Sharp accompany them, in various attitudes of Afro jazz-fusion. The last song, "Amelle," sung in English by African voices, is the closest the album comes to a true melding of two cultures, but the album does speak of a real journey and a musical exchange at a time when world music was not a widespread phenomenon.

The band's version of *Tusk*'s "Walk a Thin Line," with Hawkins' pleasingly hazy vocal and guest overdubs by George Harrison, was a true winner, but the album was not a commercial success. (The same went for the 1983 follow up, *I'm Not Me*, which was intended to be recorded in Brazil but ended up being tracked at Fleetwood's L.A. home.) The true wonder of *The Visitor* is that Fleetwood and Dashut had the spirit to take on—and see as an adventure—the logistical hell ride of recording in topsy-turvy Ghana so soon after the high-end roller coaster ride of touring *Tusk*. It was typical of Fleetwood's communal approach to music. Bob Brunning ran into him at a festival in 2002, where his old Blue Horizon label mates Chicken Shack were playing. "He'd remained very tight and close with Chicken Shack; he and Andy Sylvester were very good mates. We wandered around and had a couple of beers and talked about old times. Mick, with other musicians, just isn't a big star—he just isn't like that."

Nicks's first solo album, *Bella Donna*, recorded in 1980 and released in 1981, turned out to be the real follow-up to *Rumours* (and perhaps to *Hotel California*, too). Her need for an outlet for her songs—other than the three songs every two years that she recorded for Fleetwood Mac—was eventually accepted by the band as being the main reason for her starting a parallel solo relationship with Modern Records, a distant cousin of Reprise. This offshoot of Atlantic Records was formed by Danny Goldman and Paul Fishkin, and Nicks's album was its first release. The album's success must have diconcerted some among the Fleetwood Mac ranks, but Nicks was back the next year to do the group thing. As we now know, Ms. Nicks is not a quitter.

Bella Donna is an album that stands up well to the passage of time. She chose her collaborators wisely, and it's here that her pre-*Rumours* roots come through. Produced by Jimmy Iovine, who had produced two of her favorite recent albums, Tom Petty's *Damn the Torpedoes* and Bruce Springsteen's *Darkness on the Edge of Town*, it has its Gothy chiffon moments, and some really great campy rock. Her duet with Tom Petty on his "Stop Dragging My Heart Around" was a resounding radio hit. If it was true that Nicks couldn't cut a rock vocal when she was with Fritz, she could certainly blast one out now. But the real beauty of the album shows us Stevie Nicks, the lost lady of bluegrass, a sister to Dolly Parton, with the same heartfelt sincerity and melodic truthfulness. She included her gorgeous 1973 composition "After the Glitter Fades" as an acknowledgment of the continued presence of her grand-father A.J., to whom the album is dedicated.

But Nicks is too much of a wanderer to be a Nashville artist, and her musical travels echoed the uprootings of her youth, moving from city to city. The closer, "The Highwayman," is a country-rock classic, which she wrote as an intentionally romantic paean to rock's modern-day troubadours, such as the Eagles. It was her way of painting them in the best possible light—which was just so Stevie, putting highlights in the darkness of the soul.

The collection also carried with it one of rock's more whimsical song title stories: "The Edge of Seventeen" was a title before it was a song, inspired by Nicks mishearing Mrs. Tom Petty's southern accent pronouncing "the age of seventeen." Nicks told Jane Petty right away that it was going to be a song on her album, and she was as good as her word. She had hit singles with "Stop Dragging My Heart Around" and "Leather and Lace," a duet with old flame Don Henley, which charted in the United States, outshining the performance of "Tusk." And it came to pass that Stevie Nicks became the Queen of all Rock, just in time for the debut of MTV.

At the same time, Buckingham was at work on his solo, *Law and Order*, which reached the stores in early 1982. Yet again, Buckingham managed to completely distance himself from his previous release—*Tusk*. "Bwana" sets the tone for this Crazy Little Thing Called Lindsey, where Dion DiMucci meets Devo, busy arrangements and quirky solos on a visceral yet infectious drum and bass foundation. "Trouble" was a hit single in November 1981. More sophisticated than its sibling tracks, it's a beautiful, psychedelic "Lennon sings Hall & Oates" song, with an insinuating Al Stewart-esque open-ended melody, half-stated and lazy as can be.

Buckingham is one of rock's great pop brains and he just can't keep still: these recordings defy fashion. Those who found his *Rumours* vocals to be reverb-heavy would have been scandalized by the veritable burlesque show of echo and delay on *Law and Order*, all of it very tongue-in-cheek. Maybe. The Ricky Nelson ballads of his boyhood had come back to life, all twisted and mad, as if from some David Lynchian nightmare. Sometimes this effect was downright beauteous, as in the dreamlike serenade "Shadow of the West."

Mostly it's mad sounding yet strangely pretty, with some very nice, proper singing. *Tusk* must have temporarily exorcised his grittier demons—although his vexation with the Biz and life therein is apparent in his screwball R&B screecher, "That's How We Do It in L.A." Buckingham really turns out his musical closet; the album is addictive, humorous, playful, and quite bonkers. The songs, though clearly derivative of past times, are not really pastiches, but the album does leave the impression that they were played on cartoon instruments.

After the agreed-upon break from each other, Fleetwood Mac reassembled at the Chateau D'Herouville in France—Elton John's "Honky Chateau," and a haunted chateau, at least according to Nicks, although maybe she brought her spooks with her. Here, with Dashut and Caillat, they rehearsed and recorded an album of new Fleetwood Mac songs, including Nicks's iconic "Gypsy," and the result was *Mirage*. It was definitely a child of the synthy 1980s, and it was released, and loved by many, in 1982.

One who did not love it, at least not when interviewed in 1987, was Lindsey Buckingham, but instead of citing this as a reason for leaving, he was instead inclined to hang on and leave on a better note. This was to be the comeback 1987 triumph, *Tango in the Night*. Ken Caillat, on *The Penguin*, remembers the new problem of having all the members' individual managers prowling around the *Mirage* project. When he came home from recording in Paris to mix the album in Los Angeles, he jokes that he had to "spray the studio every day to keep the managers out."

Mirage was pale and wan next to the high standards set by both *Rumours* and its boisterous offspring, *Tusk*. Rather obviously, its relative blandness was both a result of the backlash against the peculiar edges of *Tusk* and also of the main songwriters' desire to spend more time and energy on their solo work. It was this yearning for otherness that caused them to cut short the tour supporting *Mirage* after only five weeks—a mere excursion by Fleetwood Mac touring standards.

Nicks went on to release two more albums, *The Wild Heart* and *Rock a Little*, before the band met again. In this time,

Buckingham gave us *Go Insane*, and Christine McVie, now managed by John Courage, released her second solo album, *Christine McVie*, and had a hit with "Got a Hold on Me."

A frustrated Fleetwood, meanwhile, was having a temporary personal setback, declaring bankruptcy in June, 1984. He had fallen victim to his own enthusiasms, which was a drag at the time, but in retrospect, what is a life that hasn't been lived a little? He has, in his career, owned restaurants, banks, bars, a cornucopia of real estate, and even a rock 'n' roll memorabilia auction outfit. Most fittingly, as partial owner of the Bee Load company, he assumed a contract to license and distribute some of the BBC's classic radio sessions, including many recordings made by his peers during the London blues boom, although that, too, would present legal complications.

Fleetwood's financial breakdown in 1984 came at the end of a magnificent trail of spendthrift exuberance. He then endured the attentions of a prurient press that was horrified by how much cash he might have put up his nose—metaphorically speaking. His marriage to Jenny Boyd finally ended before the decade turned over, and his then-current relationship with Stevie's friend Sara Recor had endured considerable turbulence along the way.

When Christine McVie was asked to record a version of Elvis's "Can't Help Falling in Love" for a film soundtrack in 1986, she invited Richard Dashut to join her in the studio. Lindsey showed up, followed by John and Mick. This led to talk of a new album. Buckingham remembers *Tango in the Night* as having beginnings as his third solo album, which he ended up turning over to the band.

It was a robust and quite surprising return to form for the group. It had been five years since *Mirage*, and that had been something of a disappointment. Christine's song "Little Lies" and Lindsey's "Big Love" were hits on both sides of the Atlantic in 1987. The recording period, while nowhere near the mutual angstfest of *Rumours*, marked Stevie Nicks's time to have the big trouble.

Entrenched in touring another successful solo album, *Rock a Little*, she had abused cocaine and alcohol, and this had exacted a grim toll. Eventually, her management company, friends, and family staged an intervention, and she checked into the Betty Ford Clinic to clean up. Although she was not thrilled by this intervention forcing her hand, the stay at Betty Ford marked the end of her decade-long romance with cocaine. On returning to the studio, she found that her time spent touring meant that she was missing from much of the recording, and a heated band meeting followed. The issue was resolved satisfactorily, and a little more Stevie (some of it artificially manufactured) was added to prop up the harmonies, making it a bona fide Fleetwood Mac release.

Of course, that wasn't the end of the story. Buckingham, of all the band members, seemed to feel the need to establish a performing identity outside of the all-embracing Mac. It was doubtless a reaction against the forces that had just as strongly sucked him in. He was having second thoughts about touring, and he freely expressed as much. Christine joked to the press that she'd break his limbs if he didn't take to the road with them. Like Mick and John, she was of the school that believed that a tour followed an album as surely as the sun rose and set. For Lindsey's part, he preferred to be in the studio—unlike Stevie who dialed straight into the audience every night. Mo Ostin managed to persuade him to sign on for a tour of the United States but the band's celebrations were short-lived; Buckingham had third thoughts and decided that this was a good time to leave, with the memory of a number-one album still flushed and warm.

The ending—which was not really an ending, although it felt like one—culminated in an ugly band encounter, wherein Buckingham lost his temper in an altercation with Nicks. In interviews conducted after the publication of Mick Fleetwood's autobiography, Buckingham has said the incident did not happen exactly as described in the book. He claims that he did not shove Nicks, and says that Nicks had even apologized to him for Fleetwood's version.

Even so, it was reportedly a tense scene. After witnessing it, John McVie told Buckingham, "I think you'd better leave." McVie later explained, he meant "leave" as in, leave the room. Buckingham left the band. As far as we know, Christine did not make good on her threat. Five and a half years later Nicks persuaded him to show up to play the acutely prestigious inauguration celebrations for newly elected President Clinton, who had used their "Don't Stop" as his campaign rally theme. Although for the band this was a rather prickly reunion, the event highlighted just how tightly Fleetwood Mac had become woven into the national fabric. They were indeed an American treasure.

Fleetwood Mac is famed for its revolving-door membership, and the 1980s and 1990s were even more dizzying in that regard than the previous two decades. After the reunions, sometime in 1998, it was Christine who left—and presumably left for good—because she said the "R" word: Retirement. At the age of 54, she sold her L.A. home, her car, and her piano and moved back to England to be with her family and friends. She would live at her country estate, a kind of Benifold-on-Caviar. It was a hugely symbolic and quite final gesture, for the band was deeply rooted in the United States. She had finally had enough of life on the road, although she did briefly appear as a guest performer on the band's 2003 all-new release, *Say You Will*.

After Christine's departure, the band did not try to replace her; they had learned their lesson from the last 20 years. It was one thing to replace Peter Green—although he was a revered figure, the band were in their early days, and their public success was nowhere near the scale of *Rumours*. Other members who came and went prior to Buckingham and Nicks joining did not attach themselves to public consciousness in the same way. The five members of the 1975 band became almost family to the world, their tortured lives laid bare for us to sing along to. We wanted them back for more, and we would accept no substitute.

Buckingham's 1987 departure had sparked all manner of speculation about who might take his place. Everyone from Don Henley to Peter Frampton was suggested, although not necessarily by the band. The new members who ended up joining after the departure of Buckingham—and of Nicks, in 1993—had a near impossible time replacing the beloved.

These artists were pedigreed members of rock 'n' roll families. Billy Burnette, who joined as a singer and writer to fill half of Buckingham's spot, is the son and nephew of 1950s rock 'n' roll stars Dorsey and Johnny Burnette. Elvis would drop by their house when Billy was a kid. Lead guitarist Rick Vito, who joined at the same time, was a coveted session player, and both men were jam buddies of Fleetwood's. Bekka Bramlett, who replaced Nicks in 1993, is the daughter of the country-blues duo Delaney and Bonnie, and Dave Mason, who joined at the same time, was a founder member of the rock band Traffic. On paper, there seemed to be absolutely no reason why these new folks shouldn't work out.

Unfortunately, 1990's *Behind the Mask*, with Vito and Burnette, failed to light the fire of old, and 1994's *Time* with Bramlett and Mason just wasn't the same. After this album, Christine announced that she would record with the band, but would not tour. Stevie and Lindsey were already long gone. But people kept asking about the exes: there was just no getting beyond that. And when the Famous Five finally got back together for the 1997 MTV special *The Dance*, the reaction was absolutely delirious. They went out on the road for 45 shows and the crowds thronged, just as they had back in the day. The only difference was, the old wounds had healed and there were no fights and tensions.

In 1998 Fleetwood Mac was inducted into the Rock 'n' Roll Hall of Fame, but that board's decision to induct "only the two classic-Mac lineups of 1968 and 1975" generated a great deal of unhappiness from some former members. Bob Welch noted that the Eagles had supposedly overridden a similar board decision to include only some former band members, and he wondered why Fleetwood Mac could not do the same. Welch, it should be noted, had sued the McVie and Fleetwood element of the band in 1994. The case was settled out of court, and both parties were bound not to discuss the case. In 1997 Welch also moved to sue Capitol Records, seeking a better accounting of royalties that he believed were due from his solo albums with the label.

Although Welch remained on cordial terms with Stevie Nicks, who had sung with him on several occasions, he and his former bandmates had not spoken since the court proceedings of 1994. The Rock 'n' Roll Hall of Fame inducted Green, Kirwan, and Spencer, along with the *Rumours* lineup. Welch believes that his time with the band was associated with gloomy memories—of struggle, of Clifford Davis, and of exile—and that he would have been excluded anyway. However, something similar could be said for Danny Kirwan, the first band member to be fired by Mick Fleetwood. In the event, Peter Green was the only pre-Buckingham Nicks member to turn up for the ceremony.

After almost three decades of superstardom, many artists find themselves removed from daily life. This does not necessarily mean there's a moral failing in their character, it's simply the way things go. More often than not, though, you will hear people say how nice, unaffected, and candid the members of Fleetwood Mac are. It's a rare achievement to be selling out stadium concerts 30 years on, making new albums, and still appearing to like each other. Well, if not like, to *need* each other, which is even better. They show how to move ahead without closing the door on the past.

Says Bob Brunning, who has known Fleetwood and the McVies for almost 30 years, "They are human, ordinary people. Christine really is very unspoiled—a very nice person. I also met Stevie Nicks and Lindsey Buckingham backstage; they couldn't have been more courteous, and they didn't know me. Well, although they knew I was the first bass player, they didn't need to be polite. And they were polite in the way only Americans can be."

He recalls a visit to London's Wembley Arena during *The Dance*'s reunion tour. At the time, he had a day gig at a London primary school. His "replacement," John McVie, was now one of rock's royalty, already on his third major comeback with the band, and really not in a position to have to worry about old acquaintances from the 1960s.

"John McVie is even more down to earth than Mick. I talked my way backstage, and I hung out with John—he's a bass player and he drinks beer, like me. He goes, 'Er, I've got a crate of beer….'" Then, later, they got on with the gig and I went home. At the time I was headmaster of a primary school. The next day, I'm in the staff room and my secretary goes, 'Oh, there's a John McVie on the phone for you.' John says, 'Just wanted to call you. I'm going back to the States today. It was nice having a laugh with you.' I said, 'Thanks, have a good trip, blah, blah.'

"I put the phone down and—everybody listens to conversations in the staff room—one of the young staff said, 'What's all that about?' I said, 'Well, that was John McVie, Fleetwood Mac, you know'—and they said, *'Somebody from Fleetwood Mac just phoned you up?!!'"*

As Stevie Nicks once said, echoing the philosophy of *Rumours* itself, "You have to stay true, because in the long run, you're gonna be with yourself."

rumours: the musical

Rumours wasn't just a popular album; it was a universal album, the nexus of rock's Parnassus and the common people. Unlike the other rock acts of the mid 1970s, Fleetwood Mac reflected both the male and the female. They were stardust, they were golden—but they were also very human, and they were not in the least embarrassed by this. They were also in the right place at the right time.

Entertainment in America had just become supersized in the new era of post-Vietnam optimism. Venues, retail outlets, and distribution networks all swelled and expanded in response to the growing and apparently endless audience, and the revenue flowed freely. Warmed by the glow of the bicentennial celebrations, America felt good about itself; it was after Watergate and before Reagan bummed out the youth of America. *Rumours* and its mega-movie peer, *Star Wars*, played out in a public, shared arena; it was the era before video, before America went indoors. It was the America before the isolation of Walkmans, when car radios blasted out of open car windows—and, as Cris Morris has pointed out, *all* the tracks on *Rumours* sounded great on car radios. This sun-warmed and leisurely America was part of the message that shipped globally with the album. It was not the political America of the 1960s; it was the new Californian version, and it promoted the politics of self, with a supporting cast of convertible cars, shiny, liberated hair, and the unquestioning expectation of more. There are few shared cultural experiences like *Rumours*, experiences that survive outside of their original time frame. So one would have to look to something entirely different—to the networked 1990s TV comedy *Seinfeld*—to find anything comparable.

Fleetwood Mac came of age at the same time as FM radio, and the band's new, adult contemporary sound was the perfect message for this newly mainstream medium. Although they were huge as a recording act, they were even better as a live entity; they came into their own in 1976 and 1977, a period when stadium rock was at the peak of its glamour. Says Ben Fong-Torres, "Ultimately, it came down to the music. It spoke to that generation. Stevie and her image matched where rock was at that time, the move to bigger stages and facilities." Similarly, the trends in radio, while maybe not benefiting the smaller, less mainstream artists, certainly worked in Fleetwood Mac's favor. Fong-Torres comments, "Rock radio on FM in the mid and into late 1970s—the corporations had taken over and had begun to present challenges to the more progressive free-form stations by doing a more formatted version that restricted the playlists and corralled the personalities."

Despite the fact that the corporations were taking over, popular music was still the common language of the post-Elvis generations. Michael Freeman ruefully remembers the day when readers couldn't wait for the music press to hit the newsstands: "There was a music press! It went all the way up from the tiny local fanzines to the national level; it was wonderful! People actually read things in those days; the papers were very influential. Good heavens, we don't have *Circus* any more—that was a great magazine."

Freeman also acknowledges that those were different times. "It's a very different scene now to that in the 1970s. Back then, there were a lot of things that had never been done, there was still groundbreaking going on, in all avenues. There was a lot of money around." The wealth of the music industry did not make the legend of *Rumours*, but it certainly helped magnify it; both in its marketing and—of more interest to their audience—in the lifestyle it afforded the artists.

It also meant that middle-tier bands like Fleetwood Mac, the blues band, were able to survive long enough to be reborn as Californian soft rockers. Says Freeman, "The bands in those days were under contracts wherein they were going to be supported for two or three records; the record companies had this vision out there where they could develop a relationship with people. These days, if a band on a major label doesn't sell a million copies, it's history; they've got one shot around. It *is* factory-like—if it doesn't work, that's it."

Bob Edwards concurs, "Back then, the pop-rock music business was still about *music*, unlike the current state of affairs which seems to revolve solely around vapid, cookie-cutter multimedia marketing opportunities."

Ironically, the recent advances in recording technology, which have significantly lowered the cost of recording and made ownership of home studios commonplace, have also taken away the cachet of the recorded song. Going into the studio is no longer the privilege of the elite and rock will never again be as glamorous as it was in the 1970s. *Rumours* was a big-screen, glorious technicolor event. The record may have been made by regular folks, down-to-earth people who happened to have made a lot of money, but it was also a drama, and it was larger than life.

The band was fortunate enough to be signed to one of the most sympathetic and respected labels of the day. Warner Brothers gave Fleetwood Mac both marketing expertise and the benefit of a good reputation. It presented the band in a suitably credible light, and the network of its vast empire meant that the album did not suffer the disappointing sales of previous pop masterpieces such as *Pet Sounds*. It also gave them creative freedom. The band trusted the label to act in their best interests, even at times when acting this way may have gone against corporate interests.

In a 1997 interview, Lindsey Buckingham mentioned trusting Warner Brother's longtime executive Russ Thyrett so much that he actually asked Thyrett if he, Buckingham, should participate in *The Dance*, the long-wished-for Fleetwood Mac reunion album and tour. He actually asked the *record company*, which stood to make hundreds of thousands of dollars from such a reunion, if it was in Buckingham's best *artistic* interests to do this! Thyrett said that yes, it was in his best artistic interests—and Buckingham had no doubt that the answer was given in the best of faith.

Mickey Shapiro remembers a difference of philosophy at the highest corporate level of record company culture that allowed for a creative lifestyle unrivaled in modern times. "Warners had a lot of wonderful people; they were people doing their jobs, but who also had a deep sense of decency. Mo Ostin's personal kindnesses shown to the group members—listen, there were times when he wasn't thrilled with things they'd said, but his attitude was, they'd earned it; they've done something here very special.

"The negotiations were always very pleasant, even though his job was to keep as much as he could and my job was to grab as much as I could for the group! I remember when we renegotiated their deal after *Tusk*, it was really pleasant. I felt like we were dealing with colleagues. I would say the same for Steve Ross, the corporate guy. I interfaced with him quite a lot because the financial implications of some of the deals we did required they have some input. I always found there was, with the corporate managers—unlike what we've seen [in recent times] with the Enrons and some of the communication companies, greed run amok—these guys weren't in the charity business, believe me. However, they conducted themselves with respect for those [creative entities] who contributed the revenues to the company that resulted in profits. They were not just revered because they were sources of revenue, but because they were doing something that was unique and special; the companies tried to create an environment where [the artists] felt cared about. They're not going to let them jump out of an airplane without a parachute, but the range of indulgence in what I would call creative experimentation and freedom was virtually limitless. It was a beautiful time."

It couldn't happen again—at a time of simultaneous innocence and indulgence; suntanning with a vengeance by day, and snorting coke with abandon by night. Also, the ultimate relationship album was fortunate enough to come along at the same time as the mainstreaming of psychotherapy—a trend that began, of course, in California.

The joy of being part of a band, Stevie Nicks has said, is to give up part of your own authority in order to belong to a great club; it may try one's patience and compassion, but one keeps at it as one does a marriage. Fleetwood Mac's fans understood this commitment and felt part of the club when they bought the album. Fleetwood Mac was family; they chose to stay together and suppress their individual needs for the greater good, almost as if they actually had no choice. It was all that important to them. And when artists show that kind of commitment to one another, their public responds; and this response came from several generations, from the band's fans from the 1960s through to today's preteens who are just discovering Stevie Nicks and the power of chiffon.

The band's candor gave the songs their deep integrity. This frankness extended to their personal lives. When Mick Fleetwood declared bankruptcy in 1984, his inclination was not to runaway and hide, he told Mat Snow. He actually considered inviting the rock press to photograph the furniture being taken out of his home. Most appealing of all was the subject matter of the songs; seeing the band members suck it up at work and at home, and not be ashamed of it— this inspired all mortals who had to deal with the same in their lives; and we could only hope we looked as good making a mess of our own lives as they did theirs.

There is still one essential thing, the *sine qua non* of the whole equation; without this element, we would be looking back on a passing cultural phenomenon, like Charlie's Angels, rather than on a classic piece of popular world culture. Writer Dave Marsh noted that the band assembled its classic pop songs in much the same way as the Beatles—a blues-based rhythm section, great harmonies, and dazzling guitar riffs—while writing within a four-minute romantic pop tradition. Warner Brothers' Derek Taylor, speaking in the late 1970s, expresses this key factor perfectly: "It was a very, very good double-sided pop record."

acknowledgments

My deepest gratitude goes to those who gave their time and memories; who trusted me with their thoughts, and who offered advice and referrals. Your generosity will always be appreciated. To Nina Bombardier, Bob Brunning, Leanne Bryan, Aneta Dubow, Bob Edwards, Kim Estlund, Ben Fong-Torres, Michael Freeman, Jeff Greenberg, John Grissim, Gretchen Heffler, Margi Kent, Al Kooper, Cris Morris, Jeff Murphy, Mark Myers, Keith Olsen, Mickey Shapiro, John Udell. Special thanks to Mike Brewer who gave so generously of his archives.

I am also very grateful to the editors at Unanimous and the Chicago Review Press for their invaluable advice and guidance—Laura Kesner, Linda Gray, Simon Majumdar, and Yuval Taylor.

Finally, a heartfelt thank you to my partner Kerry Kelekovich for his advice and boundless consideration during the long months of research and writing.

The albums *Fleetwood Mac*, *Rumours*, and *Tusk* have been rereleased in an expanded format, by Rhino Records. They have been remastered and now also include alternative mixes and outtakes.

After listening to *Rumours* more times than is really healthy, its magic endures. It's a testament to the journey of the band that made it—a journey of honesty and grace, of falling down and getting up again. Its popularity continues to this day. So, to Fleetwood Mac—thank you for the music.

selected bibliography

Interviews

All interviews conducted by Cath Carroll.

Bombardier, Nina (October 2003); Brunning, Bob (July 2003); Edwards, Bob (November 2003); Fong-Torres, Ben (November 2003); Freeman, Michael (October 2003); Grissim, John (October 2003); Heffler, Gretchen (November 2003); Kent, Margi (December 2003); Kooper, Al (October 2003); Morris, Cris (December 2003); Murphy, Jeff (October 2003); Myers, Mark (November 2003); Olsen, Keith (June 2003); Shapiro, Mickey (December 2003).

The online Fleetwood Mac resource *The Penguin* (www.fleetwoodmac.net) should really be in a list of its own, since it is such an unending fount of information. Marty and Lisa Adelson's website hosts original Q&A sessions, biographical information, discographies, guitar tablatures, as well as reams of archival material—and more.

Books

Brunning, Bob. *Fleetwood Mac: Behind The Masks*. London: Hodder and Stoughton, 1990.

Cornyn, Stan with Paul Scanlon. *Exploding: The highs, hits, hype, heroes, and hustlers of the Warner Music Group*. New York: Harper Collins, 2002.

Dannen, Fredric. *Hit Men*. New York: Vintage, 1991.

Dawson, Dinky with Carter Alan. *Life On The Road: The incredible rock 'n' roll adventures of Dinky Dawson*. New York: Billboard Books, 1998.

Fleetwood, Mick with Stephen Davies. *Fleetwood: My life and adventures in Fleetwood Mac*. New York: William Morrow and Company, Inc, 1990.

Fong-Torres, Ben. *The Hits Just Keep On Coming: The history of top 40 Radio*. San Francisco: Backbeat Books, 2001.

Hoskyns, Barney. *Waiting For The Sun: Strange days, weird scenes and the sound of Los Angeles*. New York: St. Martin's Griffin, 1996.

Kooper, Al. *Backstage Passes and Backstabbing Bastards*. New York: Billboard Books, 1998.

Smith, Joe. *Off The Record: An oral history of popular music*. New York: Warner Books, 1998.

Articles

Budofsky, Adam. "Mick Fleetwood." *Modern Drummer* (June, 2003).

Clarke, Steve. "Mick Fleetwood: Self-managed Mac." *NME* (January 28, 1978).

Crowe, Cameron. "The True Life Confessions of Fleetwood Mac." *Rolling Stone* (March 24, 1977).

DeMann, Bill. "War and Peace and Fleetwood Mac." *Performing Songwriter* (May, 2003).

Diehl, Matt. "Fleetwood Mac." *Interview* (June, 2003).

Dunn, Jancee. "Stevie Nicks." *Rolling Stone* (May 14, 1998).

"Eyewitness: *Rumours*" *Q* (May, 1997).

Forte, Dan. "Lindsey Buckingham." *Musician* (June, 1981).

Goldberg, Michale. "Lindsey Buckingham: Lonely Guy." *Rolling Stone* (October 25, 1984).

Grabel, Richard. "Fleetwood Mac in New York." *NME* (December 1, 1979).

Grissim, John. "Big Mac. Two All Gold Albums On a Star-Crossed Success Bun." *Crawdaddy* (November, 1976).

Halbert, James. "The Rumour Mill." *Classic Rock* (June, 2003).

Holdship, Bill. "Out Of The Cradle and Into The Blue." *BAM!* (May, 1992).

Jackson, Blair. "Warren Zevon's Werewolves of London."
Mix (April 1, 2000).

Lanham, Tom. "Mac Daddy." *Guitar One* (June, 2003).

Love, Courtney. "Blonde on Blonde." *Spin* (October, 1997).

Marsh, Dave. "Big Mac: Over 8 Million Sold." *Rolling Stone*
(December 1, 1978).

Martin, Gavin. "The Saga Continues." *The Sunday Express*
(October 3, 2003).

McLane, Daisann. "Five Not So Easy Pieces." *Rolling Stone*
(February 7, 1980).

Robinson, Lisa. "Stairway To Excess." *Vanity Fair*
(November, 2003).

Salewicz, Chris. "The Group As Group Encounter." *NME*
(January 19, 1980).

Simmons, Sylvie. "Macramé Goddess." *Creem, Special Edition*
(Fall, 1982).

Snow, Mat. "Debauchery! How Fleetwood Mac Survived It."
Q (May, 1990).

Sutcliffe, Phil. "Take It To The Limit" *Mojo* (December,
2003).

"Talking About Each Other: The women of Fleetwood Mac." *Glamour Magazine* (September, 1987).

Tosches, Nick. "Who Killed The Hit Machine?" *Vanity Fair* (November, 2002).

Williamson, Nigel. "Five Go Mad." *Uncut* (May, 2003).

index